IMAGES
of America

DETROIT'S INFAMOUS PURPLE GANG

An old *Detroit Times* newspaper photograph shows some members of the Purple Gang awaiting arraignment on extortion charges as a result of their involvement in the Cleaners and Dyers War of 1925 to 1928. From left to right are (first row) Abe Burnstein, Irving Milberg, Harry Keywell, and Joe Miller; (second row) Raymond Burnstein, Simon Axler, Edward Fletcher, Abe Axler, and Irving Shapiro.

On the cover: Please see above. (Courtesy of Walter Reuther Library.)

IMAGES
of America

DETROIT'S INFAMOUS PURPLE GANG

Paul R. Kavieff

ARCADIA
PUBLISHING

Published by Arcadia Publishing
Charleston, South Carolina

Printed in the United States of America

Library of Congress Catalog Card Number: 2007943379

For all general information contact Arcadia Publishing at:
Telephone 843-853-2070
Fax 843-853-0044
E-mail sales@arcadiapublishing.com
For customer service and orders:
Toll-Free 1-888-313-2665

Visit us on the Internet at www.arcadiapublishing.com

In loving memory of my father, Melvin C. Kavieff

CONTENTS

ACKNOWLEDGMENTS

I would like to thank my fiancée, Rita Davis-Kramer, for her continuous support. I would also like to thank Richard and Ros Smith, H. G. Manos, the staff at the Michigan State Archives, the staff at the Walter Reuther Library at Wayne State University, Scott Burnstein, my friends and colleagues in the engineering department at Wayne State University, Penelope Morris, and Vicki Morton of Digital Retrospectives. I would also like to thank the editors and staff at Arcadia Publishing for their support and confidence in this work.

Unless otherwise noted, all images are from the collection of the author.

INTRODUCTION

At the age of six, my father sold newspapers on the corner of Beaubien and Monroe Streets, or, as it is better known, the heart of Detroit's Greektown. It was the early 1930s when this young paperboy shouted out some of the most horrific headlines of gangland activity the city had ever experienced. Six decades later, he shared his memories, and I was completely captivated. What did not occur to me at the time was how large of an impact these stories would eventually have. During my first year of college, I embarked on a historical crusade that in many ways changed my life. Not only was I beginning to uncover the inner workings of one of America's most significant and ruthless underworld organizations, I was also cultivating a partnership with a crime historian by the name of Paul R. Kavieff.

I first met Kavieff in the early 1990s when he was authoring his book *The Purple Gang*. At the same time, I was developing a feature-length screenplay on Detroit's most notorious gang. I remember feeling overwhelmed and somewhat intimidated with his incredible wealth of knowledge in both the fields of social deviance and organized crime. There was no question that he was the foremost authority on the Purple Gang, and I needed to bring him on board in order to write and produce the most accurate depiction possible. My challenge was to persuade this expert to take a chance on an unproven screenwriter. Well, much to my surprise, he saw in me the same passion he had for this incredible story. He agreed to join the project, and for that I will always be grateful.

Detroit's Infamous Purple Gang is Kavieff's latest work on the Purple Gang and will no doubt visually preserve a part of American history that will be discussed and debated by scholars and novices alike for years to come. Now, for the first time ever, a book chronicles the most complete photographic collection of these predominantly Jewish gangsters. The Purple Gang, led by the four Burnstein brothers, Abraham, Joseph, Raymond, and Isadore, was responsible for over 500 unsolved murders. Their brutal methods of persuasion established the gang's unsavory reputation as hijackers, extortionists, and bloodletters.

The story began at the dawn of the 20th century, when the core group of Purple Gangsters spent their formative years on the chaotic streets of Detroit's lower-east side. This impoverished area filled with immigrants looking to walk down the country's golden-paved streets found the American dream to be nothing more than a fallacy. What they found was a lifestyle of hard work and little pay. The young Purple Gangsters did not seem to subscribe to the notion of honest work. As juveniles, they robbed local merchants, victimized street peddlers, and rolled drunks for easy pocket change. Their petty crimes escalated to more violent and erratic behavior, bringing nearby residents to live in a constant state of fear.

On May 1, 1918, Michigan's statewide Prohibition law went into effect. It became illegal to commercially sell, manufacture, transport, or consume alcohol. Detroit became the first city in the country with a population of over a quarter of a million to go dry. Prohibition gave birth to the modern-day bootlegger, gangster, and gunman.

Charlie Leiter and Henry Shorr, two larger-than-life racketeers who owned and operated the Oakland Sugar House, took advantage of the state's newly passed dry law. The Oakland Sugar House was an operation that sold corn sugar and brewing supplies to bootleggers and alley brewers. Leiter and Shorr recruited Joseph, who had become the street leader of the young Purple Gangsters, to assemble as a group of strong arms to muscle in on the larger alley brewing operations. The objective was to hijack the ready-made liquor, then dilute, rebottle, and sell it for enormous profits.

While the Sugar House Gang was controlling the Detroit streets, Abraham, the oldest of the Burnstein brothers, was making a name for himself in Detroit's flourishing gambling industry. It was in the Detroit casinos where Abraham, who ran many of the table games, developed important underworld and upperworld contacts. These relationships proved to be instrumental in implementing a plan that he put into action. He was going to set up a system that supplied alcohol throughout the United States once the 18th Amendment to the constitution was ratified. Abraham needed enforcement for the plan to work and partnered with the Oakland Sugar House to establish an organization for that purpose.

This newly formed underworld unity soon seized control of the city's alley breweries and hijacked booze being smuggled across the Detroit River from other gangs. They also developed large credit lines with Canadian distillers. It was illegal to sell or consume liquor in Ontario, Canada, in the 1920s but not to export it. Abraham's Purple Gang was ready and so, too, was the rest of the country when national Prohibition went into effect on January 16, 1920.

As the Purple Gang's dominance grew, so did its operations, stemming into prostitution, narcotics, and betting parlors. During the late 1920s the gang controlled the wire service that provided horseracing information to the 700 betting parlors throughout the city. These handbooks had to pay protection money to the gang and a monthly fee in order to have access to the wire service. The Purple Gang had reached the pinnacle of power by 1930 and appeared to be invincible. Witnesses to crimes were terrified to testify against anyone reputed to be a Purple Gangster. In September 1931, however, everything seemed to unravel. An intergang dispute resulted in the murder of three Purple Gangsters by members of their own gang. The three victims had violated the underworld code by operating outside the territory allotted them by the Burnstein brothers. This incident came to be known as the Collingwood massacre.

Although the Purple Gang remained in power until 1935, jealousies, egos, and intergang conflicts eventually caused them to self-destruct. The gang's place in American history and its mystique continue to live on some 70 years later.

So kick off your shoes, sit back in your easy chair, and let Kavieff take you through this fascinating journey of images.

H. G. Manos
Writer, director, producer

One

ORIGINS OF THE
PURPLE GANG

The Purple Gang began as a juvenile street gang in the years preceding World War I. This group of approximately 18 to 20 young men terrorized the old Hastings Street neighborhood of Detroit's lower-east side. The inhabitants of the area and the parents of the young gangsters were, for the most part, recently immigrated eastern European Jews. Many of the youngsters that formed the original Purple Gang met at the Bishop Ungraded School on Winder Street. This group of delinquents, which included Harry and Lou Fleisher, Sam Davis, Joseph and Raymond Burnstein, and the Keywell brothers, often ran errands for older underworld characters. These adult mobsters sometimes ran crap games in the Bishop schoolyard during the summer months. The original juvenile Purple Gang also engaged in rolling drunks, extorting money from other children, and forcing street peddlers to pay protection money. If the money was not forthcoming, carts were overturned, and fruit, bread, and other wares were destroyed along with the tenuous livelihood of the huckster. It has been theorized that the Purple Gang's colorful name evolved during this period, when two Hastings Street shopkeepers referred to these delinquents as being "off color" or "purple." In all likelihood, the name was invented by a local journalist during a period of gang activity known as the Cleaners and Dyers War. The Purple Gangsters were used as muscle to force Detroit cleaners and dyers into a racketeer-controlled trade association. For those who refused to join this organization, plants were destroyed, truckloads of clothing hijacked, and purple dye was sometimes thrown on laundry. The advent of statewide Prohibition in Michigan on May 1, 1918, and national Prohibition on January 16, 1920, catapulted these juvenile gangsters into real underworld power. Working for older mobsters Charlie Leiter and Henry Shorr, the young gangsters developed their skills as hijackers, hooligans, strong-arm men, extortionists, and murderers.

Charles Leiter, seen here around 1920, and Henry Shorr were older Detroit mobsters who mentored members of the juvenile Purple Gang in hijacking, extortion, and other underworld skills. These two men were the secret owners of a legitimate corn sugar and brewing supply outlet known as the Oakland Sugar House. During this period, the young Purple gangsters were often referred to as the Sugar House Gang.

Shorr, seen in this early 1920s mug shot, and Leiter controlled the Oakland Sugar House through legitimate front men. Shorr was the "bag" or payoff man for the Sugar House Gang. He also had very good connections with the New York and Chicago mobs. Both Shorr and Leiter were experts at setting up alley breweries. These were complete brewing plants installed in old barns and warehouses. Shorr disappeared in December 1934.

The Old Bishop School, seen here in a 1935 photograph, was located on Detroit's lower-east side. The building actually housed two separate schools, a regular kindergarten through eighth grade school and a vocational school for delinquents. It was here that the original Purple Gang got its start in the years 1916 to 1918.

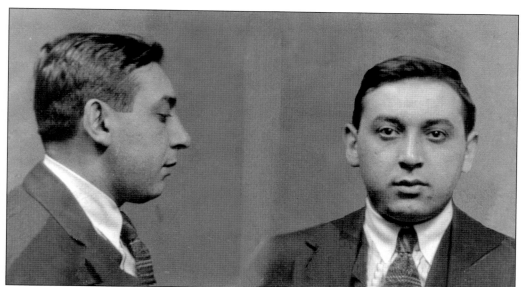

Abraham Burnstein was the reputed leader of the Purple Gang. This Detroit police mug shot was taken in 1920 after Burnstein was arrested on suspicion of homicide. Burnstein, with his three brothers, Joseph, Raymond, and Isadore, formed the leadership faction of the Purple Gang during the mob's heyday, from 1927 to 1932. By 1920, Abraham was a respected and well-known Detroit underworld figure.

Joseph Burnstein was picked up on suspicion of armed robbery at the time of his first arrest in 1917. He was the second oldest of the Burnstein brothers. He was considered one of the toughest and most cunning leaders of the Purple Gang during their golden era, from 1927 to 1932. It was his business sense and reputation for ferocity that made him a major force behind the Purple Gang's rise to dominance.

Raymond Burnstein, shown early in his underworld career, developed a reputation as a "shtarker," or strong-arm man, while still a youngster at the Old Bishop School. Raymond and Joseph were the chief enforcers for the Purple Gang. Raymond also operated a popular Detroit resort known as the Kibbutzer Club.

Isadore Burnstein, in this photograph from about 1925, was the youngest of the four Burnstein brothers. He lived in the shadow of his older brothers. Isadore worked in the Purple Gang's handbook and wire service operations in the late 1920s. He later left the Detroit area and moved to California with his brother Joseph.

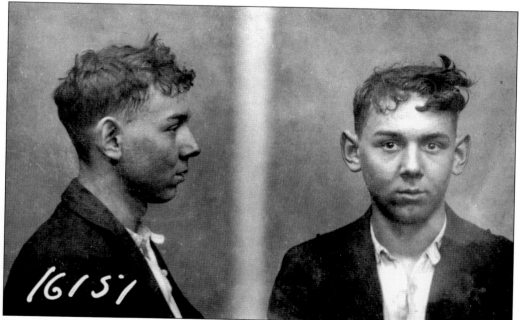

Harry Fleisher, in an early Detroit police mug shot, was better known in the Detroit underworld as "H. F." He was a close friend of Joseph Burnstein and a notorious Purple Gang lieutenant. Harry was known for "doing his own work," or never hiring anyone to kill for him. He was greatly feared and respected in the Detroit underworld.

Louis Fleisher, pictured here as a federal prisoner in 1927, was a younger brother of Harry Fleisher and one of three Fleisher brothers. He is pictured here in a mug shot taken shortly after his first conviction for hijacking a truckload of tires. He got his start in the juvenile Purple Gang and spent most of his life in and out of prison.

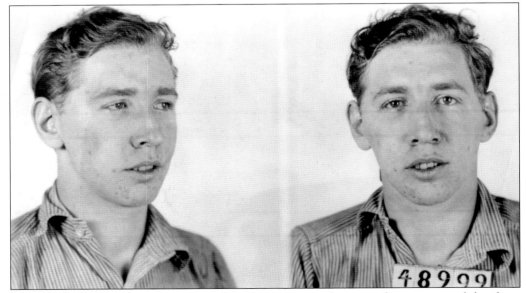

Sam Fleisher, shown here in an early federal prison mug shot, was the youngest of the three Fleisher brothers. He received his first conviction for operating an illegal still with his brother Harry in 1936. Sam was known for his quick temper and his ability with a gun.

Sam "Fatty" Burnstein was a member of the juvenile Purple Gang and was no relation to the Burnstein brothers. His sister Bella was Harry Fleisher's first wife. Another sister was married to Louis Fleisher. During the 1920s, Sam ran blind pigs for the Purple Gang. In later years, he worked with Louis as a safecracker. He is pictured in this photograph taken around 1936.

Philip Keywell, shown in a 1928 mug shot, and his younger brother Harry were both associated with the juvenile Purple Gang. Philip worked as a lieutenant of the Burnstein brothers in the late 1920s. He had the reputation of being a very dangerous gunman. In 1930, local law enforcement won its first serious victory over the Purple Gang when Morris Raider and Philip were convicted for murdering a 17-year-old boy.

Harry Keywell, seen in this 1927 mug shot, was Philip Keywell's younger brother. He was also a lifelong friend and partner of Purple Gang boss Raymond Burnstein. Harry was convicted of first degree murder for his part in the Collingwood massacre on September 16, 1931. He was sentenced to life in prison at the age of 20.

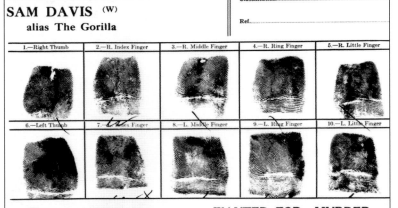

DETROIT POLICE DEPARTMENT

SAM DAVIS (W)

alias The Gorilla

Classification............................

Ref.............................

1.—Right Thumb	2.—R. Index Finger	3.—R. Middle Finger	4.—R. Ring Finger	5.—R. Little Finger
6.—Left Thumb	7.—L. Index Finger	8.—L. Middle Finger	9.—L. Ring Finger	10.—L. Little Finger

WANTED FOR MURDER

This Department holds warrant for Sam Davis, alias The Gorilla, for the murder of Harry Gold, whom he shot about 12:30 A.M., February 17, 1932, in the left chest and left abdomen during an attempted hold-up. He was dead upon admittance to Receiving Hospital.

DESCRIPTION: Jewish; age, 24; 5 ft. 4 in.; 140 lbs.; florid complexion; protruding lips; hazel eyes; light brown hair.

Warrant is also for John Doe (no description) and for Nate Karp. See Circular No. 3383 for description of Nate Karp.

Wire all information to

JOHN P. SMITH,
Superintendent of Police,
DETROIT, MICHIGAN.

Circular No. 3384.
April 5, 1932.

Homicide File No. 2573.

Sam Davis was known in the underworld as "the Gorilla" because of his simian profile and his proficiency as a strong-arm man and extortionist. His lack of mental ability was compensated for by his great physical strength. A small man in stature, he was nonetheless feared for his determined ferocity. Among other jobs, he was suspected of participating in the murder of Sugar House Gang boss Henry Shorr in 1934.

Sam Siegel was an Oakland Sugar House Gangster who worked with Charles Leiter and Henry Shorr in the early 1920s. He was known as an extortionist and a muscle man. Siegel distanced himself from the Sugar House mob once the younger Purple Gangsters dominated the operation. (Courtesy of the Central Records Division, Michigan State Police.)

Irving Shapiro was also known as "Little Irv" and "Bow-legged Charlie." He was a very tough Purple Gang enforcer who made a name for himself during the Cleaners and Dyers War of 1925 to 1928. He was greatly feared in the Detroit underworld where he divided his time between shaking down blind pigs and working as a gunman. He was murdered in July 1929 when he argued with his partners over the division of loot from a kidnapping ransom.

Abe Rosenberg, shown here in state prison, was also known as "Buffalo Harry" because he was originally from Buffalo, New York. In 1916, he was convicted of armed robbery in Detroit. After getting out of prison, he worked for the Purple Gang as a pimp and enforcer. He was also a suspect in the 1945 murder of state senator Warren Hooper. (Courtesy of the State of Michigan Archives.)

Zigmund Witkowski was known in the underworld as Ziggie Selbin. Selbin was a vicious Purple Gang gunman. He once admired a ring that he noticed a man wearing at a blind pig. He offered to buy the ring. When the man refused, Selbin clubbed him unconscious and tried to remove the ring. When this failed, he produced a knife and cut off the man's finger. He was shot to death in 1929.

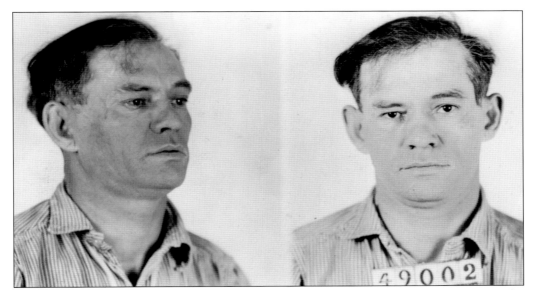

Jack Selbin was sometimes known as "Yonkel the Pollack." Jack was Ziggie's stepfather and a career criminal. He was one of the mentors of the juvenile Purple Gang. By the late 1920s, Selbin was one of the bosses of the "little Jewish navy" faction of the Purple Gang. The little Jewish navy owned several boats and occasionally ran liquor into Detroit from Canada. The Purple Gang was much better known as hijackers.

Abe Kaminsky, also known as "Angel Face," is shown here in a 1918 photograph. Kaminsky was a strong-arm man and extortionist who sometimes worked for the Sugar House Gang. A career criminal, his tactics lacked polish. He would walk into a blind pig and demand money from the operator by holding a knife to his throat or sticking the barrel of his pistol in his victim's mouth. His tactics were both crude and effective.

There was a great deal of ethnic cooperation in the Detroit underworld, as can be seen in this late 1920s group mug shot in which Abe Kaminsky was picked up with a group of Detroit-area mafioso. He was involved in a bootleg whiskey deal when rounded up by Detroit police. Kaminsky is seen here, number 26157.

Morris Raider was a Purple Gang lieutenant whose specialty was jewel theft and bank robbery. This mug shot was taken in 1918 after he was convicted of automobile theft. In 1930, Raider was convicted of manslaughter in the Arthur Mixon murder case. He had directed Philip Keywell to shoot an unarmed youngster after an argument outside a Purple Gang liquor cutting plant. (Courtesy of the State of Michigan Archives.)

Harry Altman, pictured in this 1935 mug shot, was also known as "Two Gun Harry" and "the Indian." He was a Purple Gang enforcer who was handy with a knife or a gun. Altman was often used by the Purple Gang as a collector. Despite his colorful street names, he was known for brawn and not brains. He died in a Michigan state prison of cirrhosis of the liver in 1950.

Abe Zussman (right) was a professional assassin and drug dealer. This photograph was taken by Detroit police in 1928. Zussman was known in the underworld as "Abie the Agent." He liked to work with a knife. A favorite tactic was to follow a victim into a theater, take a seat behind him, and when the audience applauded, Zussman would run a stiletto through the back of the seat.

Pictured at far left in a late 1920s Detroit Police Department group photograph, Abe Zussman was picked up with a group of underworld characters on suspicion of kidnapping. Kidnapping other wiseguys, especially wealthy gamblers, was a popular business.

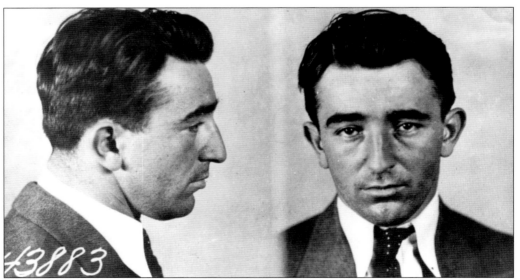

Harry Sosnick was also known as "Harry the Hat" because he always wore a pearl gray fedora. Sosnick grew up with the core group of Purple Gangsters. A minor underworld figure, he ran night clubs in Detroit, Chicago, and Florida. His biggest claim to fame is that he was married and divorced 16 times.

Jack Wolfe was the Oakland Sugar House Gang accountant. He kept the books and ran the Sugar House outlet. As an employee and associate of Charlie Leiter and Henry Shorr, he was depended on to keep two sets of ledgers. One ledger was for the federal inspectors and Prohibition agents. The other was to keep track of supplies sold to the thriving alley brewing business.

Louis Achtman was a Sugar House Gangster who sometimes worked as a gunman for Leiter. He also worked as a truck driver delivering bootleg supplies to alley breweries. He was a mentor to the young Purple Gang on hijacking jobs.

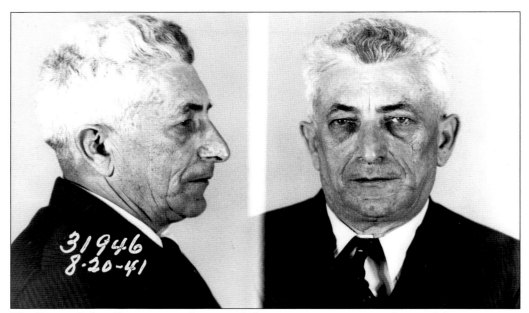

The Detroit Police Department often rounded up gangsters at various phases of their careers to take a current mug shot. Willie Laks, seen in a 1941 mug shot, was an old country criminal who had served time in Russian prisons before arriving in the United States as a young man. Laks was associated with the Sugar House Gang and often worked with the younger Purple Gangsters in various racket schemes.

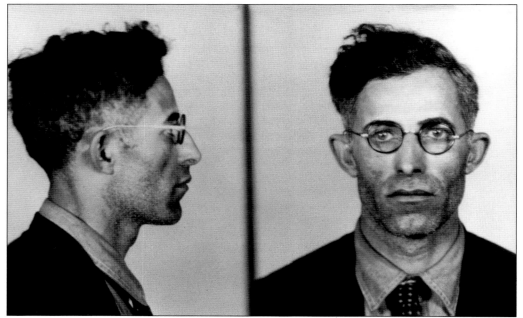

Jacob Levites worked in the Oakland Sugar House as a clerk and stock man. He also assisted Charlie Leiter in the design and installation of Purple Gang brewing and cutting plants. Levites was a good mechanic and was also often used by Leiter to keep his trucks and personal vehicles in good working order.

Shown in a 1928 mug shot, Earl Passman was a Purple Gang associate and sometimes bookkeeper. He was shot to death in 1931 by Harry "the Indian" Altman as the result of a practical joke. Passman and another Purple Gangsters had jokingly locked Altman in a closet after he had walked in to get his coat. As the two men held the door shut, Altman yelled for them to let him out or he would start shooting. Thinking he was not serious, they laughed. Suddenly, Altman pulled a pistol and fired through the door, striking Passman in the chest. Not knowing what to do, the two men carried Passman's body out of the apartment and left it in an alley.

Jack Redfern was an Oakland Sugar House mob enforcer. He often worked with the younger Purple Gangsters hijacking liquor. He was a dandy and a ladies' man. He was also a dangerous gunman who killed on the slightest provocation.

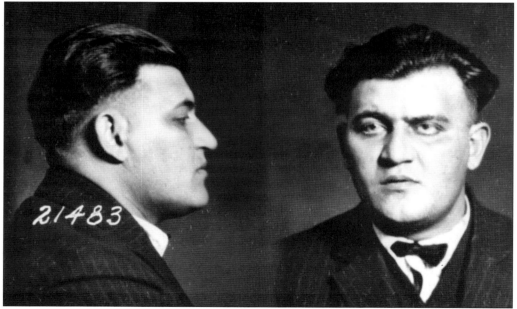

Isadore Schwartz, in this photograph from about 1923, was a lieutenant of Oakland Sugar House Gang boss Charlie Leiter. He was known as a fearsome enforcer. Schwartz was a tough, intelligent man who was an early mentor of the juvenile Purple Gang. He later developed some very good state-level political connections. (Courtesy of the State of Michigan Archives.)

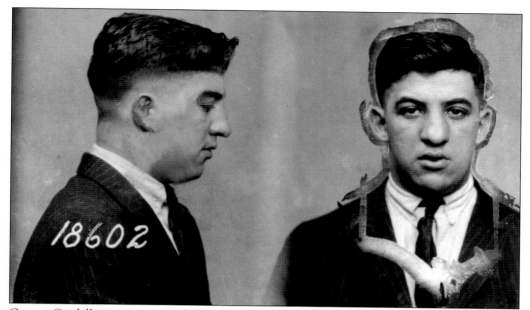

George Cordelli sometimes used the name Cordell. He was a member of the juvenile Purple Gang. He worked for the Burnstein brothers in the late 1920s as a collector. He often slashed the faces of gamblers who were late in paying back money owed to the Purple Gang. In later years, Cordelli worked for the local mafia as a very successful bookmaker. He is seen here in a 1923 mug shot.

Isadore Kaminsky was a Sugar House Gangster who was often referred to as "Uncle." His nephew sometimes did work for the Sugar House Gang. Kaminsky was one of the bosses of the early Sugar House mob. Like Charlie Leiter and Henry Shorr, he was a mentor of the Purple Gang. (Courtesy of the Central Records Division, Michigan State Police.)

Sam Abramowitz was a long time Purple Gang associate who was later involved in the 1945 plot to murder state senator Warren Hooper. Known as a freelance stickup man and extortionist, he sometimes worked as muscle for the Purple Gang. He was often used by Harry Fleisher in various shakedown schemes. This is his 1928 Detroit police mug shot.

Pictured in this police photograph from about 1928 are some of the key members of the Oakland Sugar House Gang. From left to right are Jack Redfern (32560); Harry Fleisher (16151); Charles Leiter (32564); Henry Shorr (10278); Al Russel (24687); Ben Marcus (4780); Isadore Kaminsky (29286); and Louis Achtman (32562). By the time this photograph was taken, there were approximately 200 mobsters associated with the Sugar House and Purple Gangs.

Two

A ROAD TO POWER

The young Purple Gangsters perfected their underworld skills as hijackers, extortionists, and gunmen working for the Oakland Sugar House. By the mid-1920s, the Purple Gang divided its time between working for Leiter and Shorr and hiring themselves out as guards for wealthy Detroit gamblers. In 1925, Abraham Burnstein and Francis X. Martel, a corrupt president of the Detroit branch of the American Federation of Labor, went into a partnership to regulate prices in the Detroit cleaning and dyeing industry. A racketeer-controlled Cleaners and Dyers Association was formed. All cleaners and dyers in the city were expected to join. If they refused, they received a visit from the Purple Gang. Over a period of several years, cleaning plants were demolished by explosives, truckloads of laundry hijacked or otherwise destroyed, drivers beaten, and at least two union agents murdered. The so-called Cleaners and Dyers War raged in the Detroit area from 1925 to 1928. The Purple Gang and Martel divided hundreds of thousands of dollars in spoils. A falling out between Martel and the Burnstein brothers led Martel into talking some local cleaners and dyers into filing complaints with the Wayne County prosecutor. This resulted in the 1928 trial of 13 Purple Gangsters for extortion. All of the Purple Gang defendants were later acquitted. This, coupled with the Milaflores massacre of March 27, 1927, gave the Purple Gang a reputation for invincibility. In 1926, a Purple Gang liquor distributor named Johnny Reid was murdered. The Milaflores massacre was the end result. Reid's murderer, a hired gunman named Frank Wright, and two associates, were machine gunned to death in the Milaflores Apartments. This was the first use of a machine gun in a Detroit underworld slaying. A freelance gunman named Fred "Killer" Burke operated the machine gun. He was accompanied by two Purple Gang associates. By the late 1920s, the Purple Gang ruled supreme over the Detroit underworld. Joseph Burnstein provided the Purple Gang with a sound financial footing by organizing the city's 700 handbooks and forcing them to subscribe to the Purple Gang–controlled wire service. During this period, local law enforcement could not get a jury to convict anyone reputed to be a Purple Gangster.

Seen here is a 1919 state prison photograph, Frank Speed and his gang were shakedown artists. They held up handbooks, blind pigs, and other underworld businesses. Speed was an Italian gangster with no Detroit mafia affiliation. In 1923, he was shot to death by Isadore Cantor. Cantor was one of the legitimate Oakland Sugar House front men. Speed had tried to extort money from the Sugar House, a lethal mistake. (Courtesy of the State of Michigan Archives.)

Sam Solomon was one of the leaders of the little Jewish navy faction of the Purple Gang. He was also a very successful bookmaker for the gang during the later 1920s. In this early 1940s photograph, he is suffering from blindness as the result of an advanced case of syphilis. He spent his senior years running a concession stand in the old post office building. (Courtesy of the Walter Reuther Library.)

Jack Stein is pictured in this 1927 photograph. By the mid-1920s, gangsters from all over the country were flocking to Detroit to cash in on the thriving black market action. Many of these gunmen were former New York gangsters like Stein, who went to work for the Purple Gang. Stein was a drug dealer with solid connections to Arnold Rothstein and the New York mob. Former New York mobsters were referred to by the Purple Gang as yorkies.

Edward Fletcher was a New York underworld character and a former prize fighter. He came to Detroit in 1925. Fletcher met and began working with another yorkie named Abe Axler. The two men became important lieutenants of the Burnstein brothers. They quickly developed a reputation as brutal Purple Gang enforcers and were greatly feared in the Detroit underworld. Fletcher is pictured here in 1926.

Abe Axler, shown in a 1928 Purple Gang group mug shot, and Eddie Fletcher became known as the "Siamese twins" of the Detroit underworld because they were inseparable. They soon achieved the dubious distinction of being Detroit's number one and number two public enemies. In November 1933, they were both murdered by fellow Purple Gangsters for misappropriating money intended to be used by the gang to buy a brewery after the repeal of Prohibition on December 5, 1933. The two men left a Pontiac beer garden the night they were murdered and were never seen alive again. An Oakland County constable found them in the back seat of Axler's new Chrysler on a lonely country road in the early morning hours of November 26, 1933. Evidently, they had been accompanied by two other men who were well known to Axler and Fletcher, as one of them was driving the car. The faces of both Axler and Fletcher were obliterated by heavy-caliber bullets fired at close range. The bodies were laid together in the backseat of the car, and as a final gesture of contempt, the killers placed Axler's hand in Fletcher's.

Pictured here around 1926, Harry Kirchenbaum arrived in Detroit in the early 1920s. He was originally from New York, where he had served several terms in Sing Sing Prison. He worked closely with Joseph Burnstein in the Purple Gang's gambling operations. Kirchenbaum had one problem—he was an opium addict. He often went on smoking binges for days at a time, leaving his business responsibilities neglected. This enraged Burnstein, who had beaten him several times and warned him to quit. During one of these confrontations, Kirchenbaum shot and seriously wounded Burnstein.

Irving Milberg was another former New York gangster who worked for the Burnstein brothers. He was known as an excellent marksman and soon became indispensable to the Purple Gang. He was convicted of first degree murder in 1931 for his role as a shooter in the Collingwood Manor massacre. He was sent to Marquette Prison, where he died during a surgical procedure in 1938. (Courtesy of the State of Michigan Archives.)

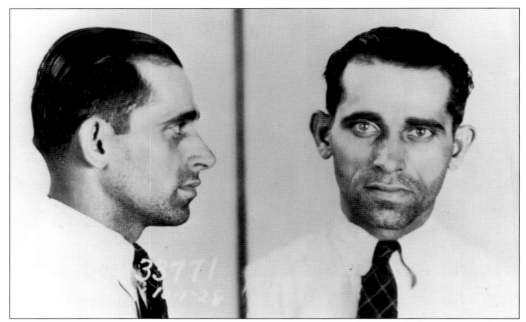

Joe Saxer was a Purple Gang gunman and enforcer who was used as muscle by the gang during the Cleaners and Dyers War of 1925 to 1928. Saxer and fellow Purple Gang gunmen were very effective at persuading local dry cleaners and tailors to join the Purple Gang–controlled wholesalers association.

Louis Rappaport specialized in kidnapping other Detroit wiseguys and holding them for ransom. Rappaport and his crew of Purple Gangsters usually targeted wealthy local gamblers. Although the Purple Gang is often credited with inventing the "snatch racket" (kidnapping), it was always just a sideline. Other Detroit underworld groups such as the Joseph "Legs" Laman kidnapping mob developed the snatch racket to a fine art.

Joseph "Honey" Miller is standing in the center of this photograph between two detectives. Miller's real name was Salvatore Mirogliotta. After killing a police officer in Kent, Ohio, Miller moved to Detroit. He quickly found employment as a gunman for the Sugar House Gang. Miller was always mentally unstable. In 1934, he was committed to a Michigan institution for the criminally insane. (Courtesy of Walter Reuther Library.)

Abe Miller was also known as Abe Stofski. He was a cousin of Joe. Both men worked for the Purple Gang as gunmen during the Cleaners and Dyers War of 1925 to 1928. After the Purple Gang extortion trial in 1928, Abe distanced himself from the gang.

Charles Auerbach was known as "the Professor." Auerbach originally came from New York where he worked as a gunman and pimp in the early 1900s. By the time he came to Detroit, he had re-created himself as a refined and educated underworld character who collected rare books. He was considered a senior diplomat and consultant to the Purple Gang. His advice was a driving force behind the Purple Gang of the later 1920s.

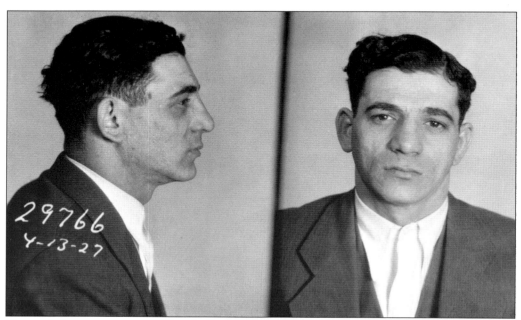

Simon Axler was a cousin of Purple Gang lieutenant Abe Axler. He worked for the gang as a gunman and enforcer in the late 1920s. Simon, like his more infamous cousin, was originally from New York City. He came to Detroit in 1925.

Simon Axler is number 29766 in this Detroit Police Department show-up photograph. This photograph also shows Harry "the Indian" Altman as number 28453. The majority of men in this group mug shot were Detroit mafioso. Purple Gangsters often worked with the Italian mob and other ethnic gangs in various rackets. There was very little rivalry between the various underworld groups. Basically anyone who could make a buck was considered okay.

This photograph of Edward Kennedy Jr. (left) and Joseph Burnstein (right) was taken during the Purple Gang extortion trial of 1928. Kennedy (no relation to the former first family) was a very successful criminal attorney who often represented the Purple Gang. Although Kennedy worked for other gangsters in the Detroit underworld, he was always considered to be the Purple Gang's "mouthpiece."

This photograph of the beautiful Marguerite Ball was taken around 1928. She was a dancer in the George White Scandals Revue. This nationally famous vaudeville act produced such stars as Lucille Ball and Ginger Rogers. Sometime in the late 1920s, she met and fell in love with Purple Gang boss Joseph Burnstein. In 1929, they were married in Detroit.

Marguerite is performing here with the George White Scandals Revue in Chicago during the late 1920s. Burnstein fell madly in love with her. They had a long and happy marriage. When he was shot in 1930, it was she who persuaded the Purple Gang boss to leave Detroit. She essentially told him that it was either her or the gang.

In 1930, Joseph Burnstein had this beautiful Tudor home built for his bride in Palmer Woods, an exclusive suburb of Detroit. The home cost more than $100,000 to build and a like amount to furnish. When asked once by a reporter where he made all of his money, Burnstein explained that he made it in a little three-chair barbershop that he owned.

Jack Budd was the bodyguard and driver for Purple Gang boss Abraham Burnstein. He was relied upon to keep his mouth shut and be dependable. Budd escorted Abraham to many high-level underworld meetings. He was known as a tough, quiet man and was well respected in the Detroit underworld. (Courtesy of the State of Michigan Archives.)

"The Two Sammies," Sam Kert (left) and Sam Cohen, were major Purple Gang liquor distributors who operated several opulent nightclubs in Detroit. The most famous was the K and C Café. The cafe was a popular meeting place for politicians, police brass, and underworld characters.

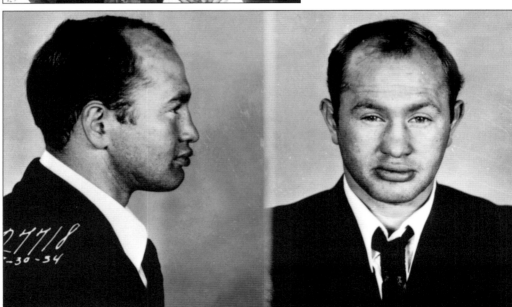

Seen in this 1934 picture, Sam "the Gorilla" Davis was a Purple Gang enforcer who got his start with the juvenile Purple Gang. Davis was always a "bug" (mentally unstable). He was committed to Ionia State Reformatory for the Criminally Insane in the late 1930s. He escaped and disappeared soon afterward. It is assumed that he was murdered by fellow Purple Gangsters who feared that he was unreliable and might talk.

Seen in this late 1950s photograph, Danny Sullivan (left) and Lincoln Fitzgerald were Prohibition-era gambling operators in Detroit. They often hired Purple Gangsters as guards in their establishments. Many Detroit-area gambling operators, including these men, were ruined as a result of the Ferguson grand jury investigation of 1940. Some went to Florida and others to Las Vegas. (Courtesy of the Walter Reuther Library.)

Johnny Reid was a former St. Louis gangster and an important Purple Gang liquor distributor in Detroit. He was murdered in 1926 as the result of a local underworld feud. His death precipitated the Milaflores massacre in March 1927 when the Purple Gang exacted revenge by killing Reid's assassin.

Patrolman Vivian Welch had a short career with the Detroit police force. He and his partner, another Detroit policeman named Max Whisman, were extorting money from Purple Gang supplied blind pigs. Whisman lost his job on the force, and Welch continued shaking down Purple Gang connected pig operators. In 1928, Welch was taken for a ride by Purple Gangsters and shot to death. He is pictured here in 1926.

Self-proclaimed Purple Gang nemesis Inspector Henry J. Garvin is shown as a young patrolman in 1915. Garvin was later head of the Detroit Police Department's crime and bomb squad. He was reputed to be on the Purple Gang's payroll throughout most of the gang's existence. In January 1930, the Detroit mafia attempted to murder Garvin. The rumor was that the inspector was extorting money from various mafioso.

Detroit patrolman Adolf Van Coppenolle is shown here around 1915. In 1930, Van Coppenolle, then a detective working with Garvin, told a police board of inquiry that the inspector did business with the underworld. The board of inquiry was investigating the attempted murder of Garvin in 1930. According to Van Coppenolle, Garvin had made promises to the Joseph "Legs" Laman mob and the mafia in exchange for information. Garvin had failed to keep his end of the deal.

Seen here in a 1953 photograph, Senior Detective Inspector Albert Shapiro started on the Detroit police force in the late 1920s and quickly developed a fearsome reputation among Purple Gangsters. He was particularly rough on Jewish wiseguys who were often administered a severe beating when arrested. These suspects were often sent through the "loop" (bounced from station to station) so their lawyers and bondsmen had difficulty finding them. (Courtesy of the Walter Reuther Library.)

The Bethune station of the Detroit Police Department was a favorite place to bring Purple Gang suspects in the late 1920s. This building was the location of the incident that precipitated the Ferguson grand jury investigation into police corruption, which began in 1939. The station is pictured in the late 1950s.

This late 1940s photograph of the old Canfield Street station house was taken shortly before the building was torn down. This station, known as the 13th precinct, was approximately three blocks west of Hastings Street and the old Jewish ghetto section of Detroit. It was in this building during the early 20th century that members of the juvenile Purple Gang were taken after they were arrested and questioned. (Courtesy of the Walter Reuther Library.)

Detroit patrolman Henderson "Ben" Turpin was photographed as a police cadet graduate in 1927. Turpin was one of the early African American officers on the Detroit police force. In 1929, he got into an altercation with Louis Bryant, a Purple Gang gunman. When Bryant asked the off-duty officer what he was looking at and pulled a pistol, Turpin shot him dead. He was later exonerated by a police board of inquiry.

Seen here around 1924, the Chesterfield Inn was one of many gambling houses operating in Wayne and Macomb Counties during the period of 1900 to 1939. Many Purple Gangsters started their underworld careers working as guards in gambling operations like the Chesterfield Inn. Large-scale gambling houses were often targets for freelance stickup men. Just having a Purple Gang gunman on the payroll was often enough to keep trouble away. (Courtesy of the Walter Reuther Library.)

Gambling house operator William Bischoff, also known as "Lefty Clark," is seen here awaiting arraignment on gambling charges. Wealthy gamblers like Clark often hired Purple Gangsters as bodyguards for personal protection against kidnappers. Detroit gangs such as the Joseph "Legs" Laman mob preyed on wealthy underworld characters. Some of the worst predators in the early Detroit underworld were actually brought to the city by local gambling-house operators to work as guards.

This photograph of the old Detroit Recorders Court building was taken in the late 1960s shortly before the structure was torn down. The building was the scene of many important underworld trials of the 1920s and 1930s. The Purple Gang extortion trial of 1928 and the Collingwood Manor massacre trial of 1931 drew crowds of spectators from all over the state. (Courtesy of the Walter Reuther Library.)

This photograph, taken during the 1928 Purple Gang extortion trial, shows from left to right, a Detroit police detective, Abraham Burnstein, and Purple Gang attorney Edward Kennedy Jr. Thirteen key members of the Purple Gang were tried for extortion in the Detroit cleaning and dyeing industry from 1925 to 1928 and for conducting a reign of terror. They were later acquitted by a jury.

Frank X. Martel, president of the Detroit Federation of Labor and reputed partner of Burnstein in the Detroit cleaning and dyeing industry shakedown, invited Chicago labor racketeers to Detroit in 1925 to establish a wholesalers association to presumably control prices in the cleaning industry. This precipitated the Cleaners and Dyers War of 1925 to 1928. Cleaning and dyeing plants and tailor shops were forced to join the association by Purple Gang gunmen or pay the consequences. (Courtesy of the Walter Reuther Library.)

Isadore Burnstein and Joseph "Honey" Miller can be seen to the immediate left of the court reporter in the center of this photograph of the Purple Gang extortion trial in 1928. Frank X. Martel was conveniently out of the city on union business. Purple Gang members were acquitted in the trial due to the fact they had better legal talent than the state.

This 1930 trial of a group of Purple Gangsters caught carrying concealed weapons is significant in that it clearly showed an unsavory connection between the Purple Gang and police inspector Henry J. Garvin. When detectives William Delisle (left) and Roy Pendergas (right) arrested the Purple Gangsters, they called Garvin, who directed them to let the gangsters go on orders of the mayor. Raymond and Isadore Burnstein appear here. (Courtesy of the Walter Reuther Library.)

Sam Garfield, shown here in the early 1960s, was a senior Detroit underworld character and a good friend of Joseph Burnstein. In the mid-1930s Garfield and Burnstein invested in Mount Pleasant oil wells. They created the Mammoth Oil Company. Some nationally known underworld bosses, including Meyer Lansky were also partners of Garfield. (Courtesy of the Walter Reuther Library.)

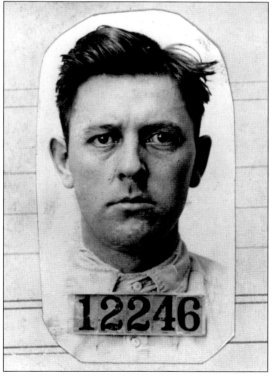

Thomas Camp, seen in this Jackson Prison mug shot around 1919, was also known as Fred "Killer" Burke. Burke was a former St. Louis gangster. He often worked for the Purple Gang in the late 1920s. He was the machine gunner in the Milaflores massacre in 1927 in Detroit. In 1929, he killed a St. Joseph police officer. He died in Michigan's Marquette Prison in 1940. (Courtesy of the Archives of the State of Michigan.)

Chicago gunman Frank "Frankie the Pollack" Wright was paid by a Detroit gangster to come to the city and murder a Purple Gang liquor distributor named Johnny Reid in 1926. After Wright killed Reid, he made the mistake of staying in Detroit. In March 1927, Purple Gangsters lured Wright and two friends to the Milaflores Apartments where they were executed in Detroit's first machine gun slaying.

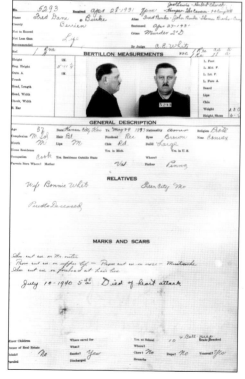

Fred "Killer" Burke's Marquette Prison register page from April 28, 1931, is shown in this photograph. Burke was convicted of second-degree murder in the slaying of a St. Joseph police officer during a traffic altercation. He was a fugitive for about a year. Burke was later captured and extradited back to Michigan. (Courtesy of the State of Michigan Archives.)

Pictured from left to right, Ezra Milford Jones, August Winkeler, and Fred "Killer" Burke were former St. Louis gangsters who often worked with the Purple Gang in the late 1920s. It is likely that Burke participated in the Chicago St. Valentine's Day massacre in 1929. A Thompson submachine gun found in his St. Joseph hideout was connected by ballistics to the massacre.

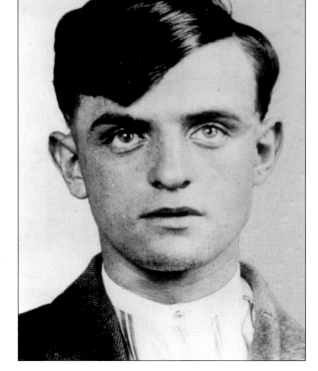

This mug shot of Ezra Milford Jones was taken shortly before he was murdered by Detroit mafioso. Jones was greatly feared by certain members of the Detroit mafia who had dealt with him in St. Louis. On June 15, 1932, Jones' luck ran out when he was shot to death in a Detroit blind pig known as the Stork Club. Jones was one of the most notorious underworld characters of the Prohibition era.

Shown here in 1932, the Stork Club on Rowena Street in Detroit was a very exclusive blind pig, one of the best in the city. It was a favorite watering hole for Purple Gangsters and other local mobsters in the late 1920s and early 1930s.

This crime scene photograph of the interior of the Stork Club was taken shortly after Ezra Milford Jones was shot to death while standing at the bar ordering a drink on June 15, 1932. Witnesses claimed that Jones came in alone and was joined by a group of Italian mobsters. This group included Pete Licavoli and Joe Massei, who were Detroit mafia soldiers with a long list of beefs against Jones.

This is a Detroit Police Department wanted circular issued in the Jones murder case. Massei was a well-known Detroit mafia associate who often worked different rackets with the Purple Gang. He later moved to Miami, Florida, where he watched over the Detroit mafia's gambling interests.

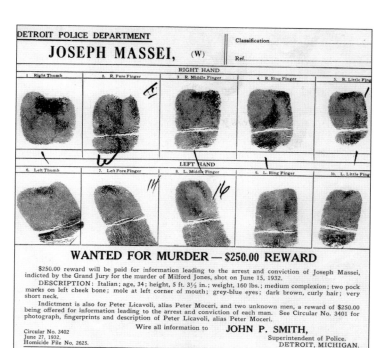

DETROIT POLICE DEPARTMENT

JOSEPH MASSEI, (W)

Classification...........................

Ref...........................

WANTED FOR MURDER — $250.00 REWARD

$250.00 reward will be paid for information leading to the arrest and conviction of Joseph Massei, indicted by the Grand Jury for the murder of Milford Jones, shot on June 15, 1932.

DESCRIPTION: Italian; age, 34; height, 5 ft. 3½ in.; weight, 160 lbs.; medium complexion; two pock marks on left cheek bone; mole at left corner of mouth; grey-blue eyes; dark brown, curly hair; very short neck.

Indictment is also for Peter Licavoli, alias Peter Moceri, and two unknown men, a reward of $250.00 being offered for information leading to the arrest and conviction of each man. See Circular No. 3401 for photograph, fingerprints and description of Peter Licavoli, alias Peter Moceri.

Wire all information to **JOHN P. SMITH,**

Circular No. 3402
June 27, 1932.
Homicide File No. 2625.

Superintendent of Police.
DETROIT, MICHIGAN.

CANCEL THE FOLLOWING CIRCULARS:
Circular, dated Jan. 15, 1932—Morris Raider—wanted for Jumping Bail Bond.
No. 3331, dated Aug. 11, 1931—Fred Eisenbeis—wanted for Murder.
No. 3341, dated Sept. 30, 1931—Harry Fleisher, alias Harry Flaisher, alias Harry Fleish, alias Harry Flaisk, alias Henry Fink—wanted for Murder.

From left to right are Detroit detective Harold Branton, Massei, attorney Edward Kennedy Jr., and detective Sgt. Albert Switzer in this photograph from 1933 taken shortly after Massei turned himself in as a suspect in the Jones murder. He was later released on insufficient evidence. Licavoli was a fugitive at this time. (Courtesy of the Walter Reuther Library.)

LOUIS GILLERMAN (DEAD) SAM VASSALLO JOHN WOLF
14418 JACOB LEVITES
21471 JOE BURNSTEIN 28205 32559 32563
25710 JAMES POWELL SAM BURNSTEIN 32561
@
SAM STEIN

A rare Detroit Police Department show-up photograph taken in the late 1920s shows Oakland Sugar House mobsters and Purple Gangsters. By the time this picture was taken, the Oakland Sugar House mob had become part of the Purple Gang. Note a very unhappy looking Joseph Burnstein third from the left.

An 1928 Detroit police photograph of key members of the Purple Gang shows Abe Axler seated in front of the group. Standing from left to right are Simon Axler, Edward Fletcher, Sam Goldfarb, Philip Keywell, Abe Zussman, Willie Laks, Harry Fleisher, and Jack Stein. By the time this photograph was taken, there were more than 200 mobsters associated with the Purple Gang.

Seen from left to right in this 1928 Detroit police show-up photograph are (first row) unidentified, Irving Shapiro, Morris Raider, and Henry Miller; (second row) Earl Passman, Frank Klayman, Joe Saxer, Fred Smith, Sam "Fatty" Burnstein, Zigmund (Ziggie) Selbin, Philip Keywell, Harry Keywell, and unidentified. The Purple Gangsters were at the height of their power when this photograph was taken.

This group of Purple Gangsters specialized in kidnapping other wiseguys, especially wealthy gamblers. These men were arrested on August 5, 1929, as suspects in the July 1929 murder of Irving Shapiro.

The Detroit Police Department once estimated that the Purple Gang was responsible for some 500 unsolved murders in the city during the Prohibition era. This unfortunate hoodlum made the dire mistake of trying to stick up a Purple Gang handbook. The Purple Gang dealt with their enemies with great ferocity. For this reason, it was very difficult for police to get a statement from witnesses.

In Prohibition-era Detroit, police officers were fair game for gunmen. This policeman walked into a drugstore while a holdup was in progress and was promptly shot through the head by escaping bandits.

Meyer Cohen, better known in the Detroit underworld as "Jew Max," was suspected of being one of a group of hijackers who stole a Purple Gang liquor shipment. He was called to a meeting with several Purple Gangsters in a downtown Detroit hotel in early 1932. Cohen thought they wanted to barter for the liquor. When the meeting was over, Cohen was shot to death.

Despite the Purple Gang's reputation for murder, associates often tried to steal from one another. This is a crime scene photograph of the body of Ben Bronstein. Bronstein was a Purple Gang associate who made the fatal mistake of double-crossing his colleagues in a liquor deal. He was taken for a ride, shot through the back of the head, and dumped in the street.

Pictured in this late 1920s photograph of Detroit Mafia gunmen, from left to right, are Pete Corrado, Thomas Licavoli, Vince Mano (seated), Joe Gaustella, Andrew Zerilli, Tony Delia, and an unidentified man. The Purple Gang often worked with the Italian mob. Most of the large-scale rum running on the Detroit River was done by the River Gang. This was the precursor to the modern Detroit mafia. Corrado became an important Detroit area-mafia boss. Licavoli took over the Toledo, Ohio, rackets.

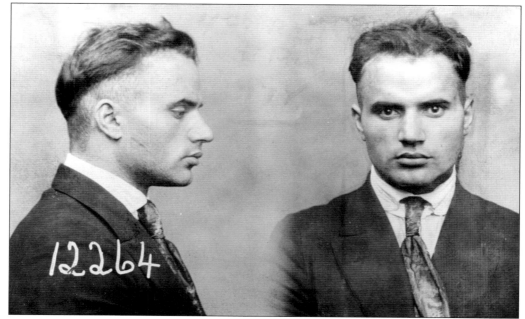

Angelo Meli, once a River Gang gunman, became a powerful mafia boss by the late 1930s. This mug shot was taken in 1919 when Meli was arrested by the Detroit Police Department's black hand squad as an extortion suspect. Meli and other Detroit mafia bosses had an amiable relationship with the Purple Gang during the gang's era of dominance.

Detroit mafia boss Joseph Zerilli went on to become one of the most powerful mob bosses in the country. He was responsible for providing Abraham Burnstein with a retirement income in Burnstein's elderly years. This was indeed a rare honor in the underworld. He is pictured here as a young gunman.

Detroit area mafia boss Pete Licavoli Sr. is shown testifying before the Kefauver investigation committee in the early 1950s. The Detroit mafia family was ruled by a consortium of bosses that included Licavoli, Zerilli, John Priziola, and several other men during the 1930s through the 1960s. Licavoli later retired to his "Grace" ranch in Arizona. (Courtesy of the Walter Reuther Library.)

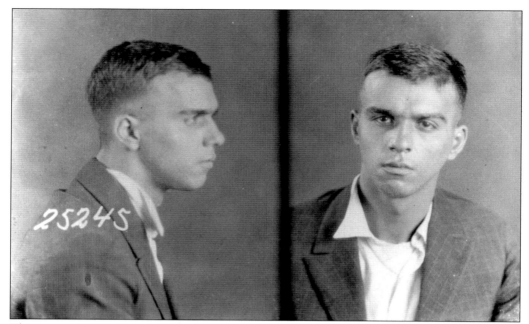

This is a mid-1920s Detroit Police Department mug shot of James Licavoli, also known as "Jack White." Licavoli was a first cousin to Pete and Thomas Licavoli. He worked as a gunman in Detroit during Prohibition. He later left Detroit for Cleveland, Ohio, where by the late 1970s, he was head of the Cleveland mafia family.

Detroit police photographed this group of mobsters associated with the River Gang. The so-called river mob did most of the large-scale rum running on the Detroit River during Prohibition. They operated north and south of Detroit and had a good relationship with the Purple Gang. Leaders of the River Gang became the founding fathers of the modern Detroit mafia.

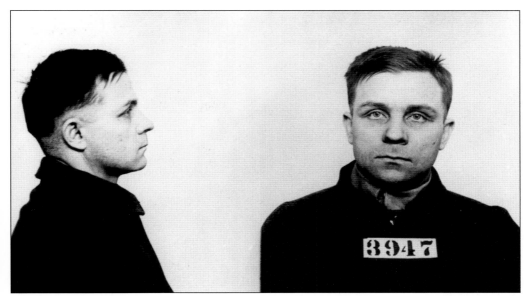

Philip "Russian Shorty" Kozak was a ruthless Hamtramck gunman and coleader of the Detroit-based Carson-Kozak mob. This group specialized in violent bank holdups. They also robbed pedestrians, gas stations, and businesses. No one was safe from groups like these. This gang was typical of the type of predators that operated in the Prohibition-era Detroit underworld. This is a late 1920s mug shot of Kozak.

James "Jimmy" Carson was the brains behind the Carson-Kozak mob. A former Great Lakes sailor, Carson drifted into crime in the mid-1920s. Carson and another member of the gang once went on a one-day crime rampage in Detroit in which they killed a police officer, shot a Hamtramck detective, robbed a bank, and totaled a stolen car. (Courtesy of the State of Michigan Archives.)

Joseph "Legs" Laman, standing between two court officers, and his mob specialized in kidnapping Detroit area wiseguys, mostly wealthy gamblers. The gang was destroyed in 1929 by a task force of state and Detroit police. Many kidnappings attributed to the Purple Gang were actually done by the Laman mob. Laman later became a state witness and exposed his former partners in return for the reduction of a long prison sentence. (Courtesy of the Walter Reuther Library.)

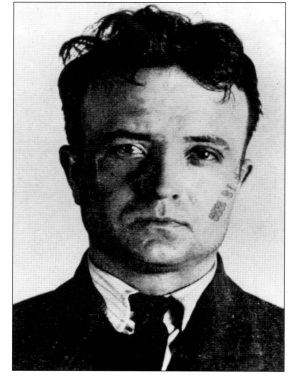

Paul Poluszynski, also known as Paul Jaworski, was the leader of a mob of bank robbers and safecrackers operating out of the Detroit area. When things got hot in southeast Michigan, the gang moved their operations to Pennsylvania, where they robbed mining payrolls. In the east, they were known as the Flathead Gang. Jaworski was executed in Pennsylvania in 1929 for the murder of a payroll guard.

Detroit mayor Charles Bowles became the only mayor in the history of the city to be recalled. The mayor was reputed to be doing business with the thriving Detroit underworld. The charges were never proven even though the recall campaign, led by popular WMBC commentator Gerald Buckley, was successful. On the night of July 22, 1930, Bowles was recalled. The recall campaign led to Buckley's murder. Bowles was a Detroit Recorders Court judge before becoming mayor. As a judge, he presided over the Purple Gang extortion trial of 1928.

Gerald Buckley was a very popular WMBC radio commentator who broadcast from a studio in Detroit's LaSalle Hotel. He considered himself a champion of the common man or "common herd," as he liked to say. Early in the morning of July 23, 1930, he was brutally shot to death by mafia gunmen as he sat reading a newspaper in the lobby of the LaSalle Hotel. This was the morning after the recall vote against Mayor Charles Bowles. Buckley, who had originally been against the recall, changed his mind and vigorously promoted it. The radio personality was supposedly doing business with the Detroit mafia. When his kickbacks from the mob were not satisfactory, he threatened to expose them on his radio show.

Three

THE COLLINGWOOD MANOR MASSACRE

The Purple Gang ruled the Detroit underworld by 1927. They controlled gambling, the local wire service, drug distribution, bootlegging, certain trade unions, and the extortion rackets. They had Detroit police brass and certain city officials on their payroll. No underworld operator did business in Detroit without kicking back money to the Purple Gang. For a short time, they were the Chicago-based Capone organization's agents for Canadian liquor. Until the late 1920s the Purple Gang also enjoyed a certain immunity from prosecution. Witnesses to crimes preferred to perjure themselves than testify against a reputed Purple Gangster in court. This immunity began to change in 1929, when a federal crackdown on Prohibition law violators ended in the convictions of several Purple Gangsters, including Abe Axler and Edward Fletcher. Their sentences, however, were light, and by 1931, they were back on Detroit streets. The seeds of destruction had been sown within the Purple Gang since the beginning. The gang members were always their own worst enemies. The egos and animosity of mobsters in their late teens and early twenties often got in the way of business. It was an intergang dispute that led to the Collingwood Manor massacre. Three gunmen, Joseph "Nigger Joe" Leibowitz, Herman "Hymie" Paul, and Isadore "Izzy the Rat" Sutker, associated with the little Jewish navy faction of the Purple Gang decided that they would no longer take orders from the Burnstein brothers. They began encroaching on the territory of other Purple Gangsters and were also creating problems with other mobs. They had to be stopped. They had served the gang well as enforcers, but they wanted their own piece of the pie. A peace meeting was set up with Purple Gang boss Raymond Burnstein at an apartment at the Collingwood Manor Apartments on September 16, 1931. The peace meeting was in reality an ambush. All three men were gunned down. This incident has often been cited as the beginning of the end for the Purple Gang.

The Collingwood Manor massacre on September 16, 1931 was an ambush disguised as a peace meeting. The body of Joseph Leibowitz is next to the sofa. Herman "Hymie" Paul's body is in the foreground. These members of the little Jewish navy faction of the Purple Gang thought they were going to get a bigger share of the action as a result of the meeting. Instead, they were shot to death by fellow gang members. (Courtesy of the Walter Reuther Library.)

This is the body of Isadore Sutker, one of three Purple Gangsters murdered in the Collingwood Manor massacre. Sutker had run down a short hallway in the apartment and tried to crawl under a bed to escape the rain of bullets. He was reported to have been shot to death by Harry Keywell. Keywell was one of three Purple Gang gunmen responsible for the September 16, 1931, massacre. (Courtesy of the Walter Reuther Library.)

From Left to right are the bodies of Sutker, Paul, and Leibowitz, casualties of the Collingwood Manor massacre. Living witness Solomon Levine later told police that Harry Fleisher killed Leibowitz, Keywell shot Sutker, and Irving Milberg killed Paul. This incident is an example of how the Purple Gang self-destructed by killing each other off. (Courtesy of the Walter Reuther Library.)

This is a crime scene investigation photograph of the alley through which the Purple Gang gunmen escaped after the Collingwood Manor massacre. The getaway car was driven by Raymond Burnstein. This scene is looking east toward Woodrow Wilson Boulevard. The upper window on the left marked X is apartment 211. The three Purple Gangsters were killed because they tried to break from the gang and start their own rackets. (Courtesy of the Walter Reuther Library.)

The Collingwood Manor Apartments are pictured here shortly after the massacre. Crime scenes often drew crowds in Prohibition-era Detroit. They were a form of free entertainment. The DeSoto sedan parked in the middle of the photograph belonged to Isadore Sutker and transported the three little Jewish navy gunmen and their associate Solomon Levine to the ill-fated peace meeting. (Courtesy of the Walter Reuther Library.)

Hymie Paul was one of three Purple Gangsters killed in the Collingwood Manor massacre. He ran the little Jewish navy handbooks. Although less lethal than his two partners, he was nevertheless an experienced gunman. This mug shot was taken several years before the massacre. (Courtesy of the Walter Reuther Library.)

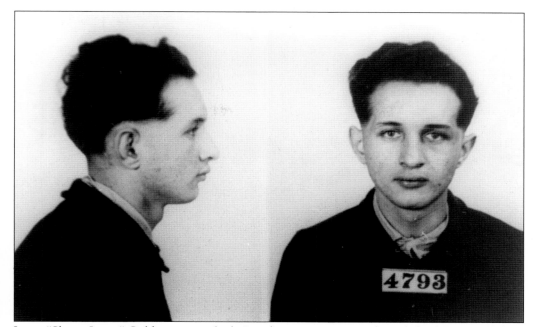

Louis "Sleepy Louie" Goldman was a little Jewish navy gunman and jewel thief. He is seen here in a 1929 Marquette Prison mug shot. Goldman's sister was married to Isadore Sutker. The little Jewish navy was a faction of the Purple Gang that has often been confused as a separate group.

Sutker and his two partners, Paul and Joseph Leibowitz, were Purple Gang enforcers who wanted to break from the gang and form their own. The three men were originally from Chicago, where they were forced out by the Al Capone mob. They went to work for the Purple Gang in 1926. They turned out to be cutthroats against their own colleagues and in their dealings with other Detroit mobs. They paid for their treachery with their lives.

Joseph "Nigger Joe" Leibowitz received his underworld moniker because of his dark skin color. He was a totally ruthless sociopath and probably the most dangerous gunman in the little Jewish navy faction of the Purple Gang. Leibowitz and his two partners were very wary as they had many enemies. Solomon Levine, an associate, arranged for their peace meeting with senior gang members at the Collingwood Manor Apartments.

Pictured in the witness box, Levine is giving a deposition about the Collingwood Manor massacre in late September 1931. Levine was both a close friend of Raymond Burnstein and a partner of the three little Jewish navy gunmen shot down in the massacre. He had been duped by Burnstein into believing he was driving Hymie Paul, Joseph Leibowitz, and Isadore Sutker to a peace meeting at the Collingwood Manor Apartments.

Defense attorneys visit the scene of the Collingwood massacre with the Wayne County prosecutor and his assistant. From left to right are Defense attorney Edward Kennedy Jr., defense attorney Rodney Baxter, Wayne County prosecutor Harry Toy, and assistant prosecutor Miles N. Cullehan. Baxter is pointing to a bullet hole in the wall. The jury was brought to the Collingwood Manor Apartments to view the scene of the crime.

The three Purple Gangster defendants in the Collingwood massacre trial are shown being taken back to police headquarters. In the center of the photograph wearing a light suit is Irving Milberg. Directly behind Milberg to the left is Harry Keywell. To Keywell's immediate right is Raymond Burnstein. The three defendants were brought to the crime scene along with the jury.

From left to right in handcuffs are Harry Keywell, Raymond Burnstein, and Irving Milberg, who is not yet out of the paddy wagon. The three Purple Gangsters are being returned from their trip to the crime scene. Detroit Police Headquarters is directly across the street. Note the heavy police guard.

Purple Gangster defendants in the Collingwood massacre case are shown being arraigned in Detroit Recorders Court. From left to right are assistant Wayne County prosecutor Miles N. Cullehan, Milberg, Burnstein, Keywell, and Purple Gang attorney Edward Kennedy Jr. on September 28, 1931.

The Collingwood massacre trial was held in Detroit Recorders Court in November 1931. In the far left with his head turned is Wayne County prosecutor Harry Toy. Across the table from left to right (first row) are defense attorney Kennedy, Burnstein, and defense attorney Rodney Baxter. Seated behind Kennedy on the left is Keywell. To Keywell's right is Milberg. (Courtesy of Walter Reuther Library.)

The assistant Wayne County prosecutor, pictured on the left, is speaking with Purple Gang boss Joseph Burnstein during jury selection for the Collingwood massacre case on October 27, 1931.

Purple Gangsters Isadore Burnstein (left), Joseph Burnstein (center), and defense attorney Edward Kennedy Jr. are seen in conversation during a recess in the Collingwood massacre trial proceedings at Detroit Recorders Court on November 4, 1931.

Purple Gangsters listen to testimony at the Collingwood Manor massacre trial in November 1931. From left to right are Joseph, unidentified, and Isadore.

The three Purple Gangster defendants in the Collingwood Manor massacre trial were photographed being sentenced after their first-degree murder convictions in November 1931. They are standing in front of Judge Donald Van Zile's bench. From left to right are Kennedy, Harry Keywell, Raymond Burnstein, and Irving Milberg. A first-degree murder conviction in Michigan is a mandatory life sentence without parole.

Purple Gangster Jacob Silverstein, also known as "Scotty," is seen here waiting to be called to testify during the Ferguson grand jury investigation in 1945. He was the Purple Gang's bookkeeper in the early 1930s. He made a record for himself as a decorated combat veteran during World War II. (Courtesy of the Walter Reuther Library.)

Larry Pollack grew up with the original Purple Gang. On September 16, 1931, he was driving his scrap truck down Woodrow Wilson Boulevard. The getaway car containing the Purple Gang gunmen fleeing from the Collingwood massacre shot out of an alley and almost rammed into Pollack's truck. At first, he identified the occupants of the car to police. He later perjured himself by changing his testimony.

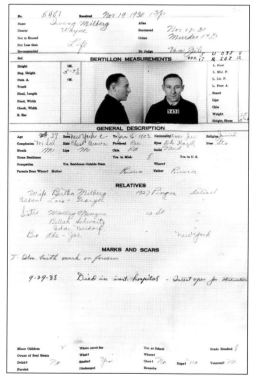

This is a picture of Irving Milberg's Marquette Prison log-in page. All inmates were mugged (photographed), fingerprinted, and had their Bertillon measurements taken upon admission to the prison. Milberg died in the prison hospital on September 29, 1938, after surgery for an intestinal blockage. (Courtesy of the State of Michigan Archives.)

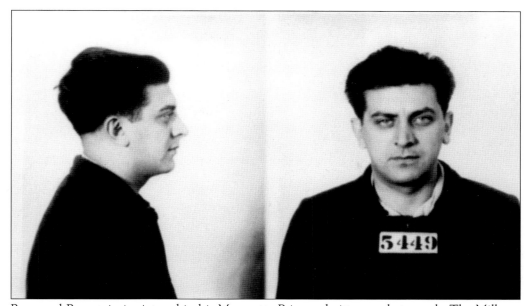

Raymond Burnstein is pictured in his Marquette Prison admittance photograph. The Milberg, Burnstein, and Keywell families spent years trying to get a new trial for the three Purple Gangsters. Soon after the only witness, Solomon Levine, had gone into hiding, he recanted his testimony. This did not help the three convicted gangsters. (Courtesy of the State of Michigan Archives.)

Harry Keywell, seen here in a 1940 Jackson State Prison photograph, and Burnstein were transferred to Jackson from Marquette Prison in the late 1930s.

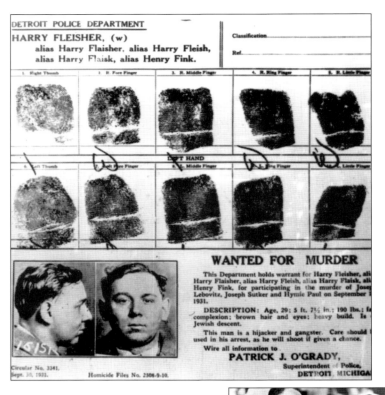

DETROIT POLICE DEPARTMENT

HARRY FLEISHER, (w)
alias Harry Flaisher, alias Harry Fleish,
alias Harry Flaisk, alias Henry Fink.

Classification

Ref.

| 1. Right Thumb | 2. R. Fore Finger | 3. R. Middle Finger | 4. R. Ring Finger | 5. R. Little Finger |
| 6. Left Thumb | 7. Left Fore Finger | 8. L. Middle Finger | 9. L. Ring Finger | 10. L. Little Finger |

LEFT HAND

WANTED FOR MURDER

This Department holds warrant for Harry Fleisher, alias Harry Flaisher, alias Harry Fleish, alias Harry Flaisk, alias Henry Fink, for participating in the murder of Joseph Lebovitz, Joseph Sutker and Hymie Paul on September 16, 1931.

DESCRIPTION: Age, 29; 5 ft. 7½ in.; 190 lbs.; fair complexion; brown hair and eyes; heavy build. Is of Jewish descent.

This man is a hijacker and gangster. Care should be used in his arrest, as he will shoot if given a chance.

Wire all information to

PATRICK J. O'GRADY,

Superintendent of Police,

DETROIT, MICHIGAN

Circular No. 3341.
Sept. 30, 1931.

Homicide Files No. 2508-9-10.

Harry "H. F." Fleisher's wanted circular for his part in the Collingwood Manor massacre is depicted here. Fleisher disappeared after the murders and, as a result, did not stand trial with his three Purple Gangster associates. In June 1932, Fleisher, accompanied by his attorney, turned himself in at Detroit Police Headquarters. By this time the only witness, Solomon Levine, could not be found. The case against Fleisher was quashed as a result.

Harry Fleisher is at the left center of this photograph. To Fleisher's right is his attorney, Edward Kennedy Jr. Fleisher and Kennedy walked into Detroit Police Headquarters and surrendered to the Wayne County prosecutor on June 9, 1932. Fleisher had been a fugitive since the massacre. During the time he was in hiding, he was a suspect in every major underworld case, including the Lindbergh kidnapping.

Four

THE ERA OF DECLINE

By 1932, the Purple Gang was well along the way to self-destruction. Between the years 1927 and 1935, 18 Purple Gangsters were brutally murdered by members of their own gang. These murders were usually the end result of arguments over the division of spoils. After 1930 and the beginning of the Great Depression, the public began to lose its tolerance for gang-related violence. The golden era of Prohibition and prosperity was almost over. Many people were out of work. The glamour of the 1920s was fading into Depression-era bread lines. On December 5, 1933, the 18th Amendment (Prohibition) was repealed. Booze was once again legal and the black market liquor business began to dry up. Organized crime groups sought out other rackets, particularly labor racketeering, gambling in the form of numbers, and drugs. Many senior Purple Gangsters were serving lengthy prison sentences. This, coupled with the murders of the Purple Gang's top enforcers and captains, caused the gang to implode. By 1935, the gang no longer controlled the lucrative wire service. According to underworld rumor, the Burnstein brothers were called to a meeting with leaders of the Detroit mafia. They were told that the Italian mob was taking over the Purple Gang's now defunct rackets. Abraham Burnstein, being the diplomat that he was and realizing that the backbone of the Purple Gang was gone, conceded. Burnstein was essentially taken care of after that by the leaders of the Detroit mafia. Individual groups of Purple Gangsters continued to operate in the Detroit underworld. Some members of a group of younger Jewish mobsters known as the junior Purple Gang began to make waves. Former Purple Gang enforcer Harry Millman led a crew of Jewish mobsters, who shook down mafia-controlled handbooks and brothels. Millman's hatred of the Italian mob was well known. For several years, Millman wreaked havoc in the Detroit underworld, protected behind the scenes by Burnstein's diplomacy. Millman was warned time and again by Burnstein to stop making trouble with the Italian mob. Millman's continued indiscretions cost him his life.

Pictured from left to right in Detroit Recorders Court on September 25, 1931, are Purple Gangsters Abe Axler, Charles "the Professor" Auerbach, Edward Fletcher, and Purple Gang attorney Edward Kennedy Jr. The three gangsters are being arraigned after their arrests under the new "public enemy law" (Disorderly Person Act), which went into effect on September 18, 1931. This was all part of a major crackdown on the underworld in the wake of the Collingwood massacre.

From left to right, this photograph shows Wayne County prosecutor Harry Toy, Kennedy, Axler, and Fletcher. Kennedy is arguing the constitutionality of the new public enemy law in front of Recorders Court judge Arthur E. Gordon. Under the new law, a conviction could be obtained on a defendant based on reputation alone. Auerbach, Axler, and Fletcher were released on bail later that day on September 24, 1931.

Axler became the first Detroit gangster to be tried under the new public enemy law on October 5, 1931. He is on the left consulting with Kennedy. On October 10, 1931, Axler was found not guilty by a jury in Judge John A. Boyne's court. The cases against Fletcher and several other Purple Gangsters were later dismissed. Auerbach was convicted on October 27, 1931. He paid a $100 fine and was released.

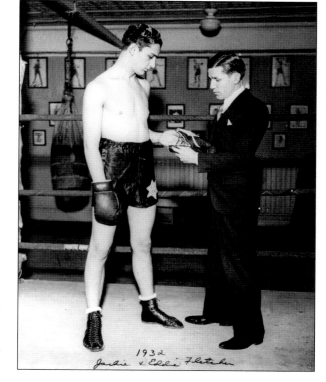

In this photograph, Jackie Sherman, a promising welterweight fighter, is on the left and Edward Fletcher on the right. After serving two years in federal prison, Axler and Fletcher were released in 1931. The pair claimed to be going straight. Fletcher worked as a fight manager for a short time. On November 26, 1933, Axler and Fletcher were murdered by fellow Purple Gangsters.

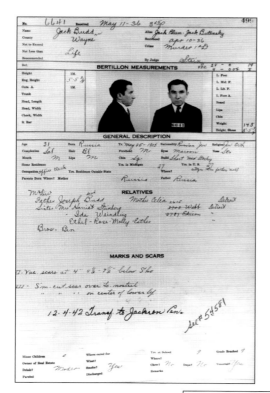

Jack Budd's Marquette Prison register page of May 11, 1936, is shown in this photograph. Budd worked as Purple Gang boss Abraham Burnstein's bodyguard and driver in the late 1920s. His first-degree murder conviction was the result of a bungled robbery in which a holdup victim was shot. (Courtesy of the Michigan State Archives.)

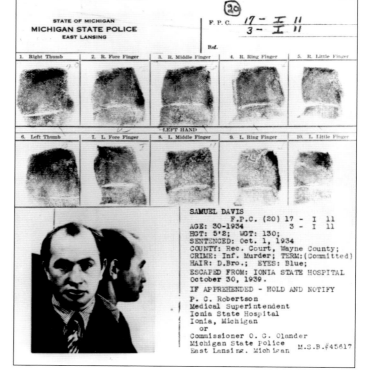

This is a Michigan State Police wanted circular for Purple Gang thug Sam "the Gorilla" Davis. Davis was sentenced to Ionia State Mental Hospital for the Criminally Insane after a first-degree murder conviction in 1934. He escaped from the hospital on October 30, 1939, and was never seen again. It is believed he was killed by former Purple Gang associates.

Purple Gangster Louis Fleisher is pictured here after his 1936 arrest in Albion. He was a suspect in an outbreak of local business safe robberies. He and his father had moved to Albion in 1935 and opened a junkyard, but in reality, the yard was a cover for a safe-cracking operation. (Courtesy of the Walter Reuther Library.)

Chester Tutha is shown here second from left with members of his Hamtramck mob known as the Lizard Gang. This predominantly Polish outfit specialized in safe cracking and bank robbery. In the late 1930s they often worked with Purple Gangsters Louis Fleisher and Sam "Fatty" Burnstein.

Louis Fleisher's supercharged 1935 Graham Paige sedan was stolen from a Ferndale dealer in 1935. Fleisher and his gang used the vehicle in safe heists. Albion police located the car in a locked garage on June 3, 1936. The firearms stacked in front were found inside the car.

Fleisher converted this stolen Graham Paige sedan into an armored car. Bulletproof glass was installed and the interior of the car was lined with steel plate. A ramp could be pulled out from under the rear of the car, which allowed stolen safes to be easily rolled into the vehicle. Safes were hauled to Fleisher's Albion junkyard and cut open.

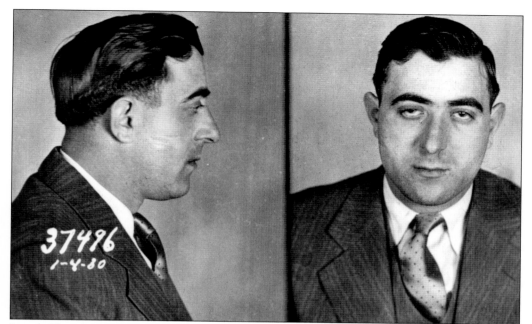

Joseph "Scarface" Bommarito was a capo in the Detroit Cosa Nostra family. He often worked with various Purple Gangsters. In the late 1930s, he went into business with Louis Fleisher and a crooked labor leader named Jack Ekelman. Using muscle provided by Bommarito, they took control of the Detroit area Master Barbers Association.

On April 28, 1938, police acting on an anonymous tip stopped Louis Fleisher's car and arrested Fleisher, Jack Sherwood, and Fleisher's wife, Nellie. Nellie tried to pitch a .38 caliber automatic pistol. Police quickly found the gun and discovered that it had been altered to fire a full clip at once. Fleisher's Highland Park apartment was searched, and police found this arsenal in a trunk.

Jack Sherwood was arrested with Louis and Nellie Fleisher on April 28, 1938. Fingerprints later identified him as Brooklyn gunman Sid Marksman, who was a fugitive for the January 13, 1938, murder of a Brooklyn, New York, poultry dealer. He was returned to New York, where he was convicted of first-degree murder. Marksman was executed in Sing Sing Prison on January 18, 1940.

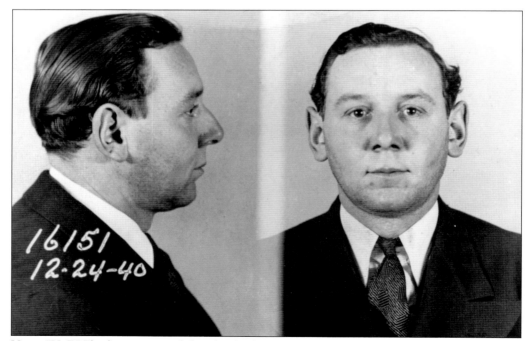

Harry "H. F." Fleisher is pictured shortly after he was released from Alcatraz in 1940. Fleisher, his brother Sam, and several other Purple Gangsters were convicted in 1936 of operating a still. As was typical with convicted Purple Gangsters, they were sent to maximum security prisons.

From left to right are Robert Goldstein, Irving Feldman, Myron "Mikey" Selik, and Solomon Isaacs, who were junior Purple Gang suspects arrested after the 1931 holdup of a downtown Detroit handbook. These young thugs were mentored by older Purple Gangsters who often used them to run errands or do minor strong-arm work.

Another group of juniors arrested during the Detroit police crackdown that followed the Collingwood Manor massacre in September 1931, from left to right, are Louis Jacobs, Robert Funkhauser, Sam Drapkin, Sam Millman, Louis Weinstein, and Louis Shapiro.

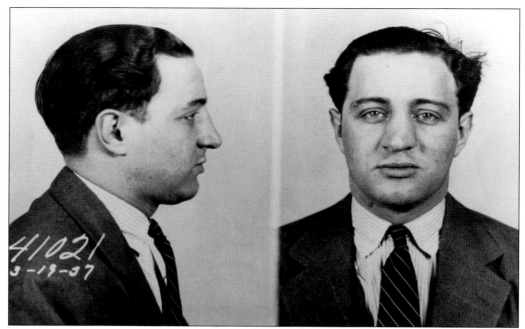

Seen here in a 1937 mug shot, Sam Millman was a younger brother of feared Purple Gang enforcer Harry Millman. He essentially lived in the shadow of his older brother. When describing Sam, one former underworld associate said, "He couldn't get out of his own way."

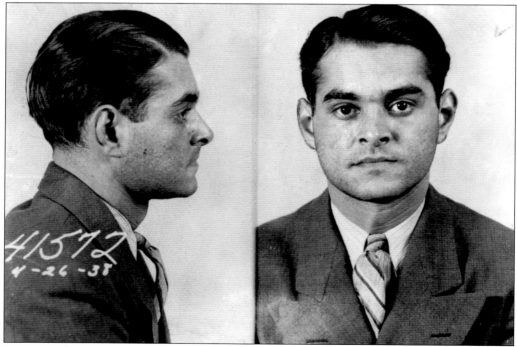

Myron "Mikey" Selik is shown following his release from prison after his first armed robbery conviction in the late 1930s. He later became a close friend and partner of Harry Fleisher.

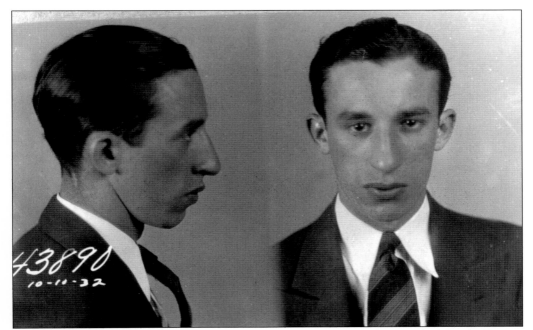

Leo "the Killer" Edelstein was a junior Purple Gang associate who later worked for the Detroit Cosa Nostra family. He was nicknamed "the Killer" because of the killing he made as a successful bookmaker.

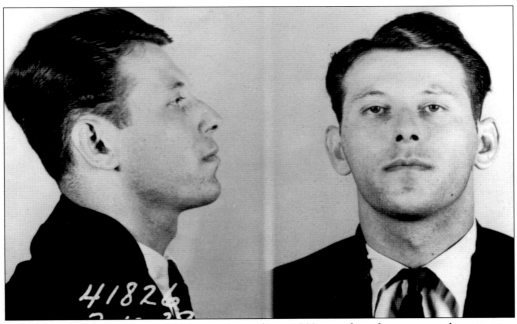

Junior Purple Gangster Irving Feldman, pictured in a 1939 mug shot, first came to the attention of older Purple Gangsters when he, Selik, and two other juniors held up a handbook. Feldman was later involved in a staged armed robbery that became the catalyst for the Ferguson grand jury investigation.

The Detroit underworld in the 1920s and 1930s was an ethnic melting pot. There was a great deal of cooperation between ethnic gangs and individuals. In this mug shot from about 1935, mafia boss Pete Licavoli (far left) appears with his predominantly Jewish partners as a suspect in an automobile theft ring.

The Oakland Baths, known as the "Shvitz," was opened at 8295 Oakland Avenue in Detroit in 1930. Built and operated by Harry Meltzer Sr., the health club and restaurant was a popular hangout for Purple Gangsters in the early 1930s. (Courtesy of the Walter Reuther Library.)

Pictured here shortly after completion in 1933, the famous Graceland Ballroom in Lupton was built by Purple Gangster Mike "One-Armed Mike" Gelfand. It was a popular hideout for Detroit gangsters on the lam. Gelfand never paid the local lumber company for construction materials. He sold the resort in 1937 and moved back to Detroit. (Courtesy of the Rose City Library.)

Junior Purple Gangster Hyman (Hymie) Cooper had the dubious distinction of being Purple Gang enforcer Harry Millman's bodyguard and driver. He is seen in a 1935 Detroit Police Department mug shot.

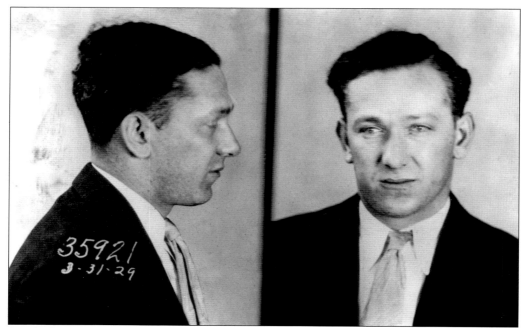

Purple Gangster Harry Sutton was one of several members convicted in 1929 of federal liquor law violations and sent to federal prison. He was an early partner of Purple Gang "loose cannon" Harry Millman. (Courtesy of the Burton Historical Collection.)

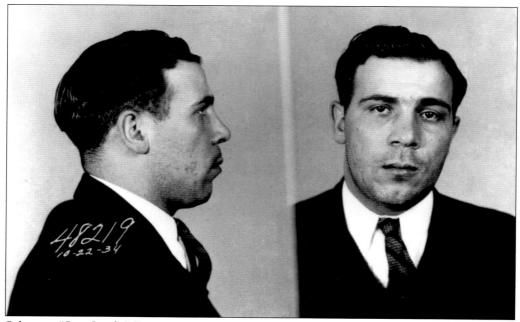

Salvatore "Sam Jacobs" Finazzo was a much-feared enforcer for the Detroit Cosa Nostra family. He was one of several gangsters who were instrumental in planning the murder of Purple Gang enforcer Millman in 1937. In later years, Finazzo was a capo and a crew leader in the Detroit mob. He is pictured here in a 1934 mug shot.

Murder Incorporated hit man Harry "Happy" Maione was one of two primary suspects in the November 25, 1937, murder of Harry Millman. When Maione was not on murder assignments, he was boss of an Ocean Hill, Brooklyn, New York, mob. Maione and a lieutenant went to the Sing Sing Prison electric chair in 1942 on an unrelated murder conviction. (Courtesy of the Municipal Archives of the City of New York.)

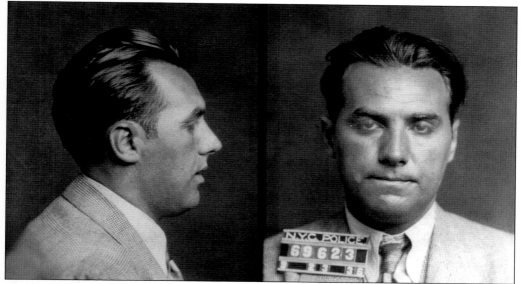

Harry "Pittsburgh Phil" Strauss was the other Murder Incorporated hit man who was a primary suspect in the 1937 murder of Millman. Strauss may be considered the worst organized crime killer in history. His estimated number of contract murders is anywhere from 30 to 200. He belonged to a predominantly Jewish underworld group out of Brownsville in Brooklyn, New York. (Courtesy of the Municipal Archives of the City of New York.)

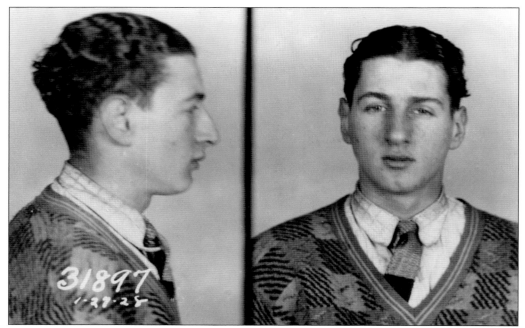

Within a few short years after this 1928 Detroit Police Department mug shot was taken, legendary Purple Gangster Harry Millman became one of the most feared enforcers in the history of the Detroit underworld.

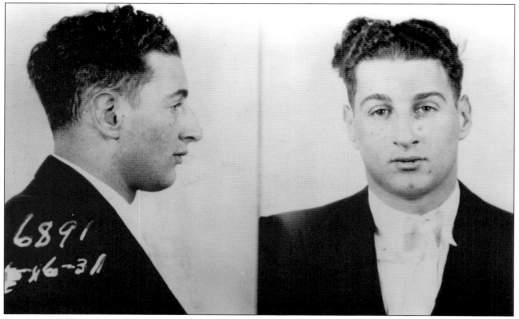

By 1931, Millman was developing a reputation for out-of-control violence, especially when he was drinking. An associate of Millman's described how he beat his girlfriend in a crowded Detroit restaurant. "You could hear a pin drop," the associate said, explaining how quiet the restaurant became during the incident.

From left to right in this photograph are Detroit Police detective Harry Schar, Purple Gangsters Harry Millman and Morris Raider, and defense attorney Neil Kelly. At this time, Raider was out of jail on appeal for a manslaughter conviction in the Arthur Mixon murder case.

By 1937, Harry Millman and his crew of former Purple Gangsters had become lone wolves in the Detroit underworld. Aside from running handbooks, Millman divided his time between shaking down mafia-protected brothels and gambling operations and busting up nightclubs owned by local mafioso. Millman was warned many times by Purple Gang boss Abraham Burnstein to stop, but Millman's hatred of the Italian mob cost him his life. (Courtesy of the Burton Historical Collection.)

Harry Millman, during one of his many arrests, is waiting to be questioned by detectives at Detroit Police Headquarters in August 1937.

This crime scene photograph of the Ten Forty Club at 1040 Wayne Street in Detroit was taken the morning after the local mafia attempted to kill Millman on August 29, 1937. A bomb planted in Millman's 1937 LaSalle coupe killed the valet by accident. The Ten Forty Club was a popular hangout for Detroit mobsters.

At approximately 2:30 a.m. on the morning of August 29, 1937, the Ten Forty Club valet went to retrieve Millman's LaSalle coupe. Ten sticks of dynamite had been wired to a sparkplug. When valet Willie Holmes tried to start the car, he was literally vaporized. The hood of the LaSalle was later found on the roof of a five-story building.

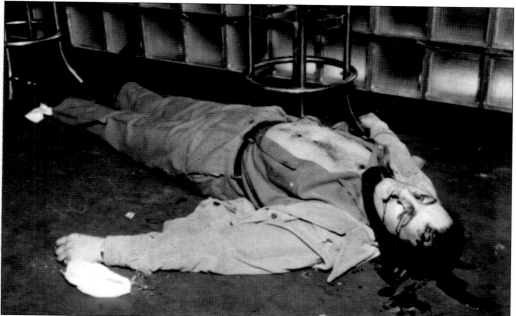

Harry Millman was shot to death before a crowd of horrified customers at Boesky's Restaurant in Detroit on November 25, 1937. Two gunmen approached Millman, who was standing at the bar, and opened fire. Millman was hit 10 times. Several other people were also shot, including Harry Gross, a partner of Millman's in the handbook business. Gross later died from his wounds.

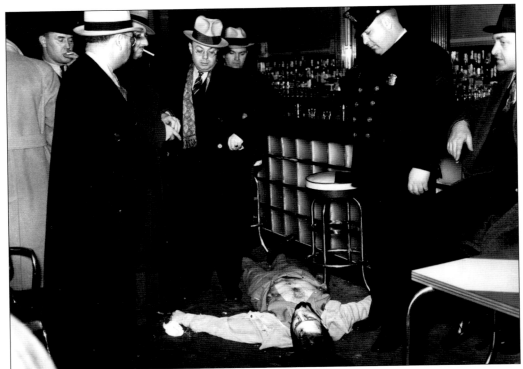

Detroit Police detectives look at the body of Harry Millman on November 25, 1937. It came as no surprise to police or anyone else in Detroit that Millman was finally murdered. After his car was blown up in August 1937, Detroit hotels stopped renting Millman rooms for fear that he would be murdered on the premises. (Courtesy of the Walter Reuther Library.)

The body of Millman is being lifted into the Wayne County coroner's hearse on November 25, 1937. It was later discovered that almost any one of Millman's wounds would have been fatal. (Courtesy of the Walter Reuther Library.)

The 1937 Ford sedan used by Millman's killers had been purchased the month before the murder in Detroit. The vehicle was abandoned by the gunmen on Ritchton Avenue the night of the murder. It was later discovered that the car was registered to a fictitious New York City address.

Harry Gross was a partner of Millman's in the handbook racket. Gross and Millman's driver, Hyman (Hymie) Cooper, were drinking with Millman the night he was murdered. Although both men dove under the table when the shooting started, they were both wounded. Gross later died from his wounds. He is seen here in a mid-1930s mug shot.

Labor leader Jimmy Hoffa and his Detroit Teamster Local No. 299 often employed former Purple Gangsters and Detroit mafioso during strikes to prevent company thugs from beating up picketing union members. This was the beginning of the International Brotherhood of Teamsters' marriage to organized crime. This is Hoffa in a February 16, 1939, police department mug shot.

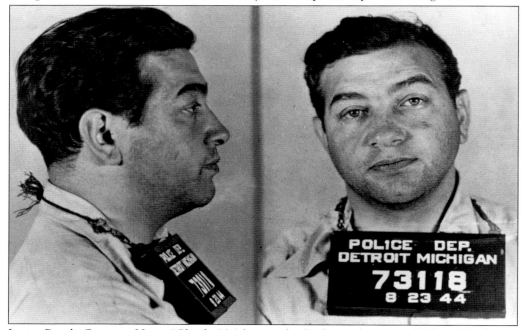

Junior Purple Gangster Harry "Chinky" Meltzer and a freelance thug named Edward Sarkesian worked together in the early 1940s. They robbed mafia-protected handbooks until Sarkesian was murdered in 1944.

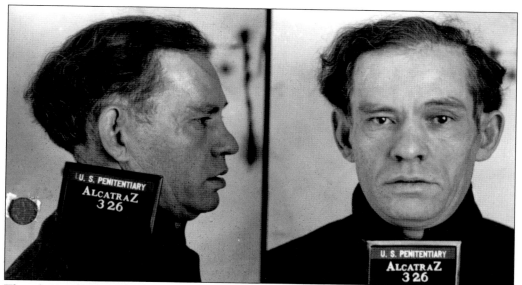

The above photograph shows aging Purple Gangster Jack "Yonkel the Pollack" Selbin in Alcatraz. The photograph below is Selbin in Leavenworth penitentiary shortly before he was released. Selbin was convicted of violating federal tax laws with Harry Fleisher, Sam Fleisher, and several other Purple Gangsters in 1936. These men were running an illegal still in Detroit. Selbin was one of the leaders of the little Jewish navy faction of the Purple Gang. Convicts were not directly released from the federal government's maximum security prison in Alcatraz. Usually shortly before their time was up, they were transferred to another federal prison and then released. (Courtesy of the National Archives and Records Administration.)

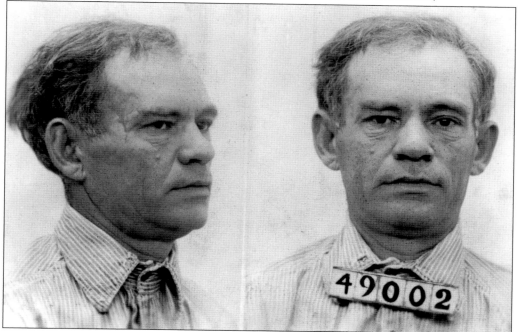

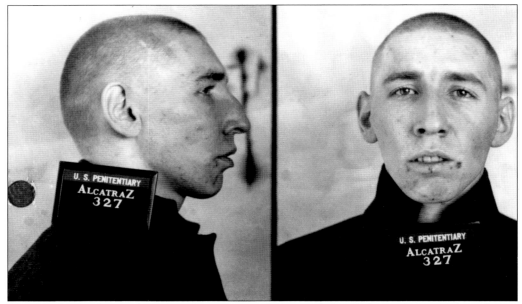

Sam Fleisher is shown above in Alcatraz around 1938 and shortly before he was released from Leavenworth penitentiary in the photograph below. All three of the Fleisher brothers served time on the infamous "Rock." Purples Gangsters were considered incorrigible and often received the harshest sentences in some of the toughest prisons. (Courtesy of NARA.)

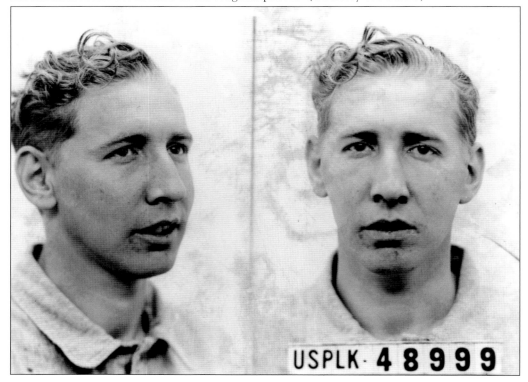

Five

THE FERGUSON GRAND JURY INVESTIGATION

The Ferguson grand jury investigation was the direct result of two incidents that occurred in 1939. The investigation exposed connections developed during Prohibition between the Detroit underworld, city politicians, and Detroit Police Department officials. It uncovered a system of graft by which the underworld was allowed to operate large-scale gambling rackets without any official intervention. The racketeers got rich and city and police officials received regular monthly protection payments. In July 1939, four junior Purple Gangsters were arrested in connection with the phony holdup of the offices of a Detroit bookmaker. The bookie, Dr. Martin C. Robinson, owed the gangsters money. He wanted them to make the payoff look like a holdup so he could get reimbursed by an insurance claim. The four holdup men were apprehended by accident by a police inspector on his way to lunch. They were brought to the Bethune station, where they bribed several police officers in an effort to get released. This precipitated an investigation of the Detroit Police Department that was quickly quashed by the department itself. Then in early August 1939, the former girlfriend of a Detroit policy house operator committed suicide with her 11-year-old daughter. Janet MacDonald had been the policy house bookkeeper responsible for seeing that graft payments to city officials were promptly paid. MacDonald had been jilted by her boyfriend. Before killing herself, she sent letters to Detroit's three daily newspapers and to the Detroit offices of the FBI. In these letters, she listed city and police department officials who were paid off monthly and how much they received. This resulted in a public outcry against corruption in Detroit government and led to the appointment of circuit judge Homer Ferguson to investigate accusations of graft being paid to city and police officials. The investigation resulted in prison terms for many, including the Wayne County sheriff, prosecutor, a former mayor, and the superintendent of police. The trials continued into the 1950s.

Judge Homer Ferguson, pictured at right with special prosecutor Chester P. O'Hara, was chosen to lead a grand jury investigation into corruption in the Detroit Police Department in 1939. The Ferguson grand jury investigation eventually destroyed major underworld gambling operations in Wayne and Macomb Counties. (Courtesy of the Walter Reuther Library.)

Junior Purple Gangsters are pictured on the first day of their trial in the Martin Robinson holdup case on January 2, 1940. From left to right are (first row) Joseph "Monkey Joe" Holtzman and Louis Jacobs; (second row) are Irving Feldman and Sidney Cooper. These four men staged a phony holdup on local bookmaker Dr. Martin C. Robinson to collect a gambling debt. (Courtesy of the Walter Reuther Library.)

This Detroit Police Department lineup photograph was taken shortly after these four junior Purple Gangsters were arrested for armed robbery on July 8, 1939. From left to right are Jacobs, Feldman, Cooper, and Holtzman. Their holdup of Robinson was one of the incidents that precipitated the Ferguson grand jury investigation.

Pictured are secretary Florence Wolfe and Robinson. Robinson talked four junior Purple Gangsters into staging a make-believe holdup at his office in order to pay a gambling debt owed to the gang. This was done so Robinson could collect on his insurance. Although he refused to file a complaint, the four Purple Gangster suspects were held by police. (Courtesy of the Walter Reuther Library.)

Detroit underworld bagman Elmer "Buff" Ryan was a casualty of the Ferguson grand jury investigation. He was the underworld character who delivered graft from gambling operators to police and city officials. The investigation was the result of an incident that occurred after the Dr. Martin C. Robinson holdup by junior Purple Gangsters. In August 1939, Janet MacDonald, a local policy house bookkeeper, sent information to the three Detroit daily newspapers and the FBI. She was in charge of keeping track of who was getting paid and how much. On August 5, 1939, she committed suicide with her 11-year-old daughter, the end result of being jilted by her policy house banker boyfriend.

Former Detroit mayor Richard Reading is being fingerprinted at Detroit Police Headquarters on April 24, 1940. From left to right are a Detroit police officer, Reading, and his son Richard Jr. Both Readings were later convicted of taking graft of as much as $4,000 a month in the late 1930s from Detroit-area gamblers. (Courtesy of Walter Reuther Library.)

Detroit Police detective Byron Farrish and his partner were assigned the Robinson holdup case. The day of the holdup on July 8, 1939, they returned an undetermined amount of the holdup money to Robinson. Farrish later claimed he did this on the order of a superior officer. Both Farrish and his partner were given some of the holdup money in gratitude by Robinson. (Courtesy of the Walter Reuther Library.)

Detroit Police detective Wilfred Brouillet and his partner, Detective Byron Farrish, were bribed by Dr. Martin C. Robinson the day of the holdup on July 8, 1939. Both officers were later brought before the Ferguson grand jury. In return for immunity, they implicated former Bethune station inspector Raymond Boettcher as having been paid $1,000 by Robinson to get the holdup money back. Both officers were discharged from the police department. (Courtesy of the Walter Reuther Library.)

Detroit superintendent of police Fred Frahm (seen here around 1940) was convicted of taking bribes from Detroit gambling operators as the result of the Ferguson grand jury investigation. Boettcher claimed that he met the superintendent in a men's room at Detroit Police Headquarters once a month, where he would hand him the payoff money. (Courtesy of the Walter Reuther Library.)

Inspector Raymond Boettcher was one of the bagmen that paid off Detroit police officials. He was given immunity from prosecution for his testimony before the Ferguson grand jury. His exposure destroyed his career. (Courtesy of the Walter Reuther Library.)

Reputed Purple Gang boss Abraham Burnstein was called in for questioning during the Ferguson grand jury investigation. His smile indicates the level of his concern. Burnstein is wiping the ink from his hands after being fingerprinted on August 14, 1940. (Courtesy of the Walter Reuther Library.)

Isadore Burnstein (left) returned to Detroit from his home in California to be questioned during the Ferguson grand jury investigation. He essentially told them nothing. (Courtesy of the Walter Reuther Library.)

Joseph Burnstein sits in Detroit Police Headquarters on August 12, 1940. All three Burnstein brothers received subpoenas to testify before the Ferguson grand jury. By this time, Joseph was well established in California. (Courtesy of the Walter Reuther Library.)

Six

THE HOOPER MURDER AND LATER YEARS

The Hooper murder was the result of an Ingham County grand jury investigation into graft in state government in 1945. Special Prosecutor Kim Sigler (later governor of Michigan) wanted to put state Republican Party boss Frank McKay in prison. McKay had very solid connections with the Detroit underworld and had been bribing various state legislators to vote certain ways on pending racetrack legislation. Some of these bills could seriously affect the pocketbooks of the Detroit mob. State senator Warren G. Hooper was brought before the grand jury and quickly caved in under the questioning of Sigler. Hooper admitted to taking bribes from McKay and agreed to become a state witness in return for immunity. As a result, McKay was reputed to have put a $25,000 contract on Hooper's life. The contract was fulfilled. Hooper was intercepted on his way home from Lansing to Albion on the evening of January 16, 1945. He was shot to death by someone riding as a passenger in his car. It was suspected from the beginning of the state police investigation into the murder that former Purple Gangsters were involved. An ex-convict who had been involved in the murder plot named Purple Gangsters Myron "Mikey" Selik, Harry Fleisher, and Sam Fleisher as the men who organized the murder plans at a meeting in Detroit in late December 1944. The Fleishers, Selik, and several others were later convicted of planning the holdup of a Pontiac gambling joint. Information about the robbery came out at the murder conspiracy trial. By 1945, most members of the old Purple Gang were dead or in prison. It was not until October 1965 that the last Purple Gang member was released from state prison.

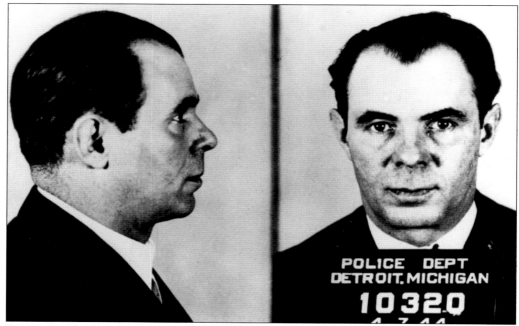

Former Purple Gangster Morris Raider is pictured around the time he was released from state prison in 1944. Raider was convicted of manslaughter in the 1930 Arthur Mixon murder case. He later became a successful realtor and builder in California.

Purple Gang gofer Sammy Abramowitz, seen here in a 1936 Marquette Prison mug shot, played an important part in the conspiracy trial of Purple Gangsters Harry Fleisher, Sam Fleisher, and Myron Selik for the murder of state senator Warren Hopper in 1945. His testimony convicted the Fleishers, Selik, and several others of conspiracy to murder in the Hooper case and of armed robbery in the Aristocrat Club extortion scheme. (Courtesy of the Michigan State Archives.)

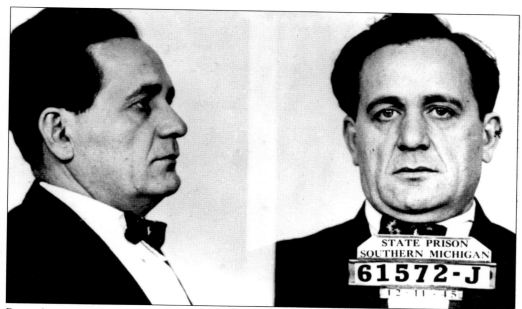

Peter Aspostapolis, also known as Pete Mahoney, was a close friend of Harry Fleisher. They were both convicted, along with several others, of conspiracy to murder in the Hooper case. Aspostapolis had the misfortune of being present when the murder plans were discussed. He was later convicted in the Aristocrat Club robbery and given an additional 25 to 30 years. He had just gone along for the ride.

Harriet "Hattie" Stocker-Fleisher was Harry's attractive second wife. She was questioned during the Sen. Warren G. Hooper murder conspiracy trial. (Courtesy of the State of Michigan Archives.)

Former Purple Gangster Harry Fleisher, seen here in a Michigan State Police mug shot, was a key suspect in the murder of Sen. Warren G. Hooper. Harry and Sam Fleisher, Myron Selik, and several associates were later convicted of conspiracy to murder and armed robbery on the testimony of Sam Abramowitz. Abramowitz disappeared in 1950.

Junior Purple Gangster Myron "Mikey" Selik and his partner, Harry Fleisher, were primary suspects in the January 1945 murder of Sen. Warren G. Hooper. Selik is pictured in a 1945 Michigan State Police mug shot.

Michigan state senator Warren G. Hooper was called before an Ingham County grand jury investigating graft in state government. Special Prosecutor Kim Sigler quickly broke down Hooper, who agreed to testify in return for immunity against Republican Party boss Frank McKay. McKay had bribed Hooper and other legislators to vote certain ways on pending racetrack legislation. Some of this legislation would have hurt the Detroit mob financially if it were passed. It was reported that McKay put up $25,000 for a contract on Hooper's life. The senator was murdered on his way home to Albion the night of January 16, 1945. Several former Purple Gangsters were suspected of killing Hooper. Hooper is pictured here in a 1944 campaign poster.

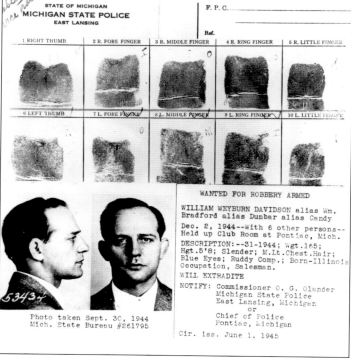

WANTED FOR ROBBERY ARMED

WILLIAM WEYBURN DAVIDSON alias Wm. Bradford alias Dunbar alias Candy

Dec. 2, 1944--With 6 other persons-- Held up Club Room at Pontiac, Mich.

DESCRIPTION:--31-1944; Wgt.165; Hgt.5'8; Slender; M.Lt.Chest.Hair; Blue Eyes; Ruddy Comp.; Born-Illinois Occupation, Salesman.

WILL EXTRADITE

NOTIFY: Commissioner O. G. Olander Michigan State Police East Lansing, Michigan
            or
        Chief of Police
        Pontiac, Michigan

Cir. iss. June 1, 1945

Photo taken Sept. 30, 1944
Mich. State Bureau #261795

This is a Michigan State Police wanted circular on William "Candy" Davidson. Davidson was an associate of Harry Fleisher and other Purple Gangsters. He was implicated in the Aristocrat Club robbery by stool pigeon Sam Abramowitz. The club was a Pontiac gambling resort for which Purple Gangsters Fleisher and Myron Selik wanted to pay them protection money. (Courtesy of the State of Michigan Archives.)

WANTED

Michigan State Police

$2,500 REWARD FOR ANY INFORMATION LEADING TO THE ARREST OF THIS MAN

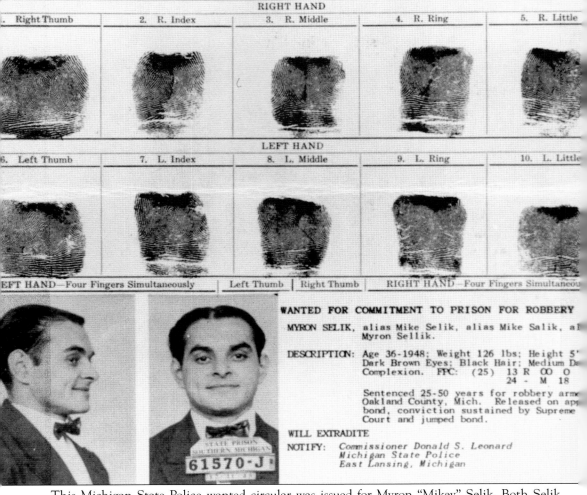

RIGHT HAND				
Right Thumb	2. R. Index	3. R. Middle	4. R. Ring	5. R. Little

LEFT HAND				
6. Left Thumb	7. L. Index	8. L. Middle	9. L. Ring	10. L. Little

LEFT HAND—Four Fingers Simultaneously | Left Thumb | Right Thumb | RIGHT HAND—Four Fingers Simultaneou

WANTED FOR COMMITMENT TO PRISON FOR ROBBERY

MYRON SELIK, alias Mike Selik, alias Mike Salik, al Myron Sellik.

DESCRIPTION: Age 36-1948; Weight 126 lbs; Height 5' Dark Brown Eyes; Black Hair; Medium Da Complexion. FPC: (25) 13 R OO O 24 - M 18

Sentenced 25-50 years for robbery arme Oakland County, Mich. Released on app bond, conviction sustained by Supreme Court and jumped bond.

WILL EXTRADITE

NOTIFY: *Commissioner Donald S. Leonard Michigan State Police East Lansing, Michigan*

This Michigan State Police wanted circular was issued for Myron "Mikey" Selik. Both Selik and Fleisher jumped their bonds in 1947. They were appealing their convictions in the Hooper murder and Aristocrat Club robbery cases. The two gangsters remained fugitives for several years. (Courtesy of the State of Michigan Archives.)

Former Purple Gangster Abe "Buffalo Harry" Rosenberg was a suspect in the 1945 murder of Sen. Warren G. Hooper.

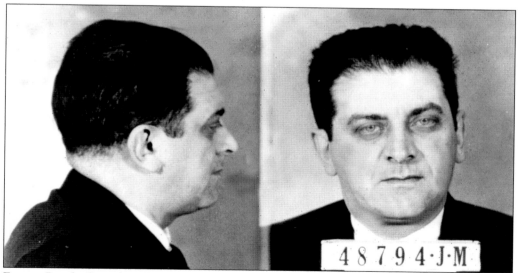

Former Purple Gang boss Raymond Burnstein is pictured in a 1945 Jackson Prison mug shot. The Purple Gang literally ran Jackson Prison in the early 1940s. It was not unusual for lifers to be let out on the weekends to go to shows or take care of other business. A crackdown in 1946 resulted in the dismissal of Warden Harry Jackson and his assistant.

This 1947 Detroit Police Department show-up photograph of Harry Fleisher was taken only days before he became a fugitive in the Warren G. Hooper case. By 1947, the Cosa Nostra family ran the underworld in Detroit. Many old-time Purple Gangsters had amiable relations with the leaders of the Detroit mafia. Gang leaders like Joseph Zerilli, Pete Licavoli, and other products of the Prohibition era had worked with Fleisher and other Purple Gang members in the old days. The man on the far right, DoDo Mazzola, sometimes worked as Fleisher's bodyguard.

In later years, Purple Gang associate David Feldman ran some of the gambling and bookmaking operations for the Detroit mafia. He is pictured in a 1931 Detroit Police mug shot.

Some important members and associates of the Detroit Cosa Nostra family are shown in 1948. From left to right are Frank Cammarata, Joseph "Long Joe" Bommarito, Joseph "Scarface" Bommarito (a cousin), Feldman, John Licavoli, and Dominic Licavoli. Jewish wiseguys were becoming a minority in the Detroit underworld of the late 1940s. Frank Cammarata was an illegal alien at this time.

By the time this photograph of former Purple Gangster and little Jewish navy boss Sam Solomon was taken in the 1950s, he had gone blind as the result of an advanced case of syphilis. In the 1930s Solomon ran one of the biggest bookmaking operations in the city. After losing his sight, he bought a concession stand in the old Detroit Post Office building that he ran for many years. Solomon operated behind the scenes during Prohibition, but was always considered the brains behind the little Jewish navy faction of the Purple Gang. Solomon's lieutenant, Mike "One-Armed Mike" Gelfand, built and operated the famous Graceland Ballroom in Lupton from 1933 to 1937.

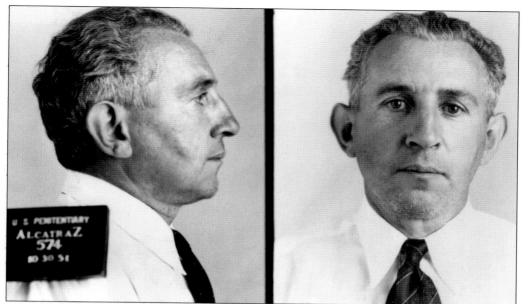

Former Purple Gangster Louis Fleisher spent most of his life in prison. The federal mug shot above was taken in 1951 when Fleisher was serving time in Alcatraz for a 1939 federal firearms conviction. Fleisher was released in 1957 after serving nearly 19 years there. He was out of prison about one year when he was caught by Detroit police attempting to blow up a cleaning establishment he was trying to extort money from. He was sent back to federal prison at Milan, Michigan, as a parole violator and then transferred to Leavenworth penitentiary, and eventually transferred back to Milan before his scheduled release. The mug shot below is Fleisher's Leavenworth photograph. Fleisher died of a heart attack two weeks before he was to be released from Milan Prison in April 1964. (Courtesy of NARA.)

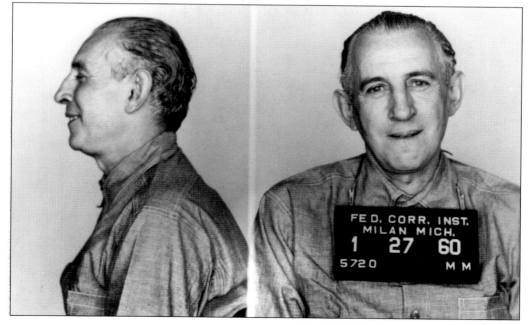

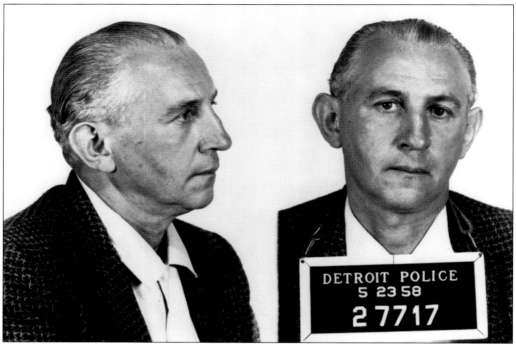

This is a 1958 photograph of Purple Gangster Louis Fleisher. This Detroit police mug shot was taken shortly after Fleisher was released after serving 19 years in federal prison.

Former Purple Gangster Harry "the Indian" Altman died in Jackson State Prison of cirrhosis of the liver shortly after this 1950 Detroit police mug shot was taken.

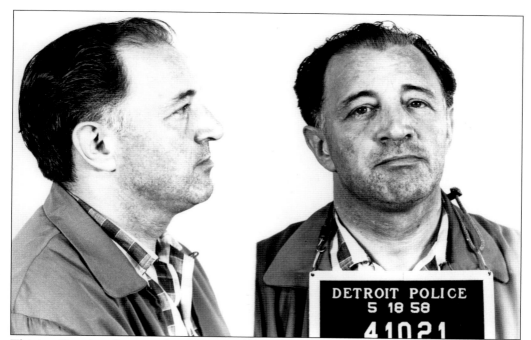

This is a Detroit police mug shot of Sam Millman taken later in his life. Millman always walked in the shadow of his older brother Harry. He served time for obstruction of justice as a result of the Ferguson grand jury investigation. He died of natural causes in 1969.

An aging Philip Keywell was a trustee at the Michigan State Correctional Facility at Jackson in the early 1950s. Keywell was a foreman on the prison farm. He lost his status when newspapers complained about the coddling of Purple Gangster convicts by prison officials.

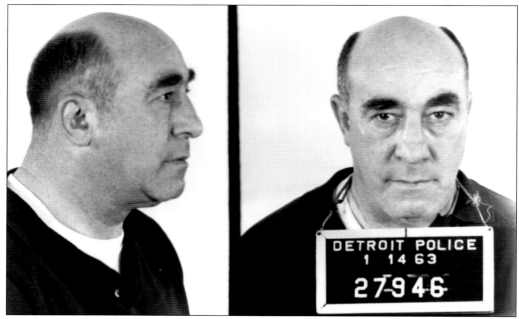

The last Detroit Police Department mug shot of Philip Keywell was taken shortly after his release from prison in the early 1960s. After many years of trying, Keywell's family finally got the governor of Michigan to commute his sentence to second-degree murder. Keywell was released in 1962 on time served as a result.

This Detroit police photograph of Hyman (Hymie) Cooper was taken in 1950, 13 years after his partner and boss, Harry Millman, met his fateful end. Cooper continued to work in the local mob numbers and handbook rackets.

14498
8-12-40

The last Detroit police mug shot of Joseph Burnstein was taken in the early 1940s during the Ferguson grand jury investigation. By this time, he had lived in California for several years. He owned racehorses, casinos in Mexico, and was a senior consultant to the West Coast underworld.

This photograph of Purple Gangster Myron "Mikey" Selik (left) and Harry Fleisher was probably taken in the mid-1940s. Both Selik and Fleisher were released from state prison in the mid-1960s. Selik continued to work for the Detroit mob. Fleisher took a legitimate job as a warehouse manager for Detroit-based Ewald Steel Company.

BIBLIOGRAPHY

Burnstein, Scott. *Motor City Mafia: A Century of Organized Crime in Detroit.* Charleston, SC: Arcadia Publishing, 2006.

Engelman, Larry. *Intemperance, the Lost War Against Liquor.* New York: Free Press, 1979.

Fox, Stephen. *Blood and Power: Organized Crime in Twentieth-Century America.* New York: William Morrow and Company, 1989.

Fried, Albert. *The Rise and Fall of the Jewish Gangster in America.* New York: Holt, Rhinehart, and Winston, 1980.

Helmer, William J. *The Gun That Made the Twenties Roar.* Toronto, Ontario: MacMillan Company, 1967.

Illman, Harry R. *Unholy Toledo.* San Francisco: Polemic Press Publications, 1985.

Kavieff, Paul R. *The Purple Gang: Organized Crime in Detroit 1910-1945.* New York: Barricade Books, 2000.

———. *The Violent Years: Prohibition and the Detroit Mobs.* New Jersey: Barricade Books, 2001.

Lynch, Dennis Tilden. *Criminals and Politicians.* New York: MacMillan Company, 1932.

Mezzrow, Milton "Mezz," and Bernard Wolfe. *Really the Blues.* New York: Random House, 1946.

Pasley, Fred D. *Muscling In.* New York: Ives Washburn Publishers, 1931.

Rudensky, Morris "Red." *The Gonif.* San Francisco: Piper Company, 1970.

Seidman, Harold. *The Labor Czars: A History of Labor Racketeering.* New York: Livernight Publishing Company, 1938.

Turkus, Burton B., and Sid Feder. *Murder Inc.: The Story of the Syndicate.* New York: Farrar, Straus, and Young, 1951.

Woodford, Arthur M., and Frank B. Woodford. *All Our Yesterdays.* Detroit: Wayne State University Press, 1969.

INDEX

DISCOVER THOUSANDS OF LOCAL HISTORY BOOKS
FEATURING MILLIONS OF VINTAGE IMAGES

Arcadia Publishing, the leading local history publisher in the United States, is committed to making history accessible and meaningful through publishing books that celebrate and preserve the heritage of America's people and places.

Find more books like this at
www.arcadiapublishing.com

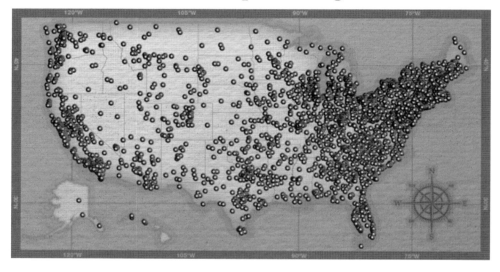

Search for your hometown history, your old stomping grounds, and even your favorite sports team.